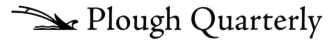 **Plough Quarterly**

BREAKING GROUND FOR A RENEWED WORLD

Autumn 2017, Number 14

Editorial: The Church We Need Now	Peter Mommsen	3
Readers Respond		7
Family and Friends		8

Feature: Re-Formation

The Spirit of Early Christianity	Eberhard Arnold	10
The Two Ways	Rowan Williams	22
Reading: The *Didache*		26
Time for a New Reformation	Jin S. Kim	32
The Unplanned Church	Claudio Oliver	38
Reading: Patient Ferment	Alan Kreider	40
Insights	Ignatius, Hermas, Polycarp	44
Re-Forming the Church	George Weigel	45

Poetry and Graphic Story

Poem: Parable	Mary M. Brown	31
Martin Luther, Renegade Monk	Andrea Grosso Ciponte, Dacia Palmerino	50

Views and Reviews

Editors' Picks		65
The Last of the First Christians	Andreas Knapp	67
Photo Essay: A Church Not Made of Cathedrals	Cécile Massie	73
Forerunners: Polycarp 2017	Jason Landsel	80

Artists: Daniel Bonnell, Jason Landsel, Randall M. Hasson, Rachel Wright, Arthur Brouthers, Andrea Grosso Ciponte, Olivia Clifton-Bligh, Malcolm Coils, Cécile Massie, Dean Mitchell

Cover: Jader Gneiting, *Old Tree, New Growth*

Plough Quarterly

WWW.PLOUGH.COM

Meet the community behind *Plough*.

Plough Quarterly is published by the Bruderhof, an international community of families and singles seeking to follow Jesus together. Members of the Bruderhof are committed to a way of radical discipleship in the spirit of the Sermon on the Mount. Inspired by the first church in Jerusalem (Acts 2 and 4), they renounce private property and share everything in common in a life of nonviolence, justice, and service to neighbors near and far. The community includes people from a wide range of backgrounds. There are twenty-three Bruderhof settlements in both rural and urban locations in the United States, England, Germany, Australia, and Paraguay, with around 2,700 people in all.

To learn more or arrange a visit, see the community's website at *bruderhof.com*.

Plough Quarterly features original stories, ideas, and culture to inspire everyday faith and action. Starting from the conviction that the teachings and example of Jesus can transform and renew our world, we aim to apply them to all aspects of life, seeking common ground with all people of goodwill regardless of creed. The goal of *Plough Quarterly* is to build a living network of readers, contributors, and practitioners so that, in the words of Hebrews, we may "spur one another on toward love and good deeds."

Plough Quarterly includes contributions that we believe are worthy of our readers' consideration, whether or not we fully agree with them. Views expressed by contributors are their own and do not necessarily reflect the editorial position of *Plough* or of the Bruderhof communities.

Editors: Peter Mommsen, Veery Huleatt, Sam Hine. Art director: Emily Alexander. Managing editor: Shana Burleson.
Contributing editors: Maureen Swinger, Susannah Black, Bernard Hibbs, Chungyon Won, Charles Moore.
Founding Editor: Eberhard Arnold (1883–1935).
Plough Quarterly No. 14: Re-Formation
Published by Plough Publishing House, ISBN 978-0-87486-834-0
Copyright © 2017 by Plough Publishing House. All rights reserved.

Scripture quotations (unless otherwise noted) are from the New Revised Standard Version Bible, copyright © 1989 the Division of Christian Education of the National Council of the Churches of Christ in the United States of America. Used by permission. All rights reserved. Article on pages 40–43 excerpted from Alan Kreider, *The Patient Ferment of the Early Church: The Improbable Rise of Christianity in the Roman Empire,* Baker Academic, a division of Baker Publishing Group, 2016. Used by permission. Back cover photograph courtesy of Yoli Shwartz / Israel Antiquities Authority.

Editorial Office	*Subscriber Services*	*United Kingdom*	*Australia*
PO Box 398	PO Box 345	Brightling Road	4188 Gwydir Highway
Walden, NY 12586	Congers, NY 10920-0345	Robertsbridge	Elsmore, NSW
T: 845.572.3455	T: 800.521.8011	TN32 5DR	2360 Australia
info@plough.com	*subscriptions@plough.com*	T: +44(0)1580.883.344	T: +61(0)2.6723.2213

Plough Quarterly (ISSN 2372-2584) is published quarterly by Plough Publishing House, PO Box 398, Walden, NY 12586.
Individual subscription $32 per year in the United States; Canada add $8, other countries add $16.
Periodicals postage paid at Walden, NY 12586 and at additional mailing offices.
POSTMASTER: Send address changes to *Plough Quarterly,* PO Box 345, Congers, NY 10920-0345.

The Church We Need Now

Why the Anabaptist vision matters

PETER MOMMSEN

This year's five-hundredth anniversary of the Reformation comes just as Christianity is undergoing what may prove to be its biggest recalibration since the fourth century. Christendom, the system in which Christianity shaped Western laws and society as the majority religion, has been shaky since the Enlightenment. Now it's in its death throes, felled by secularization, consumerism, and the sexual revolution. For better or worse, Christians must learn to be a minority. There's no better time than now to recall Karl Barth's admonition: "The church must always be reformed." What is the re-formed church we need now?

On October 31, 1517, Martin Luther famously affixed his Ninety-Five Theses to a Wittenberg church door in a brazen challenge to the authority of the pope in Rome (page 50). His action ended up sparking a religious conflict that would plunge the continent into a century of war between Catholics and Protestants. Out of the bloodshed, so runs the story, modernity was born.

For the past twelve months, festivals, films, academic conferences, and a slew of books and articles have marked the anniversary – and not just in Germany, which is awash with Luther mugs, T-shirts, and dolls, even while clergy express contrition for Luther's disastrous legacy

Malcolm Coils, *Fishing Village of Staithes, North Yorkshire*, collage with tissue paper, newsprint, and acrylic inks and paints of anti-Semitism. Pope Francis himself traveled to Sweden last year for an ecumenical service to mark the start of the Reformation 500 year. Astounding: the head of the world's 1.2 billion Catholics commemorating a man whose defiance shattered the unity of Catholic Europe.

The pope's sympathy for the rebel Luther highlights the ambiguous meaning of the Reformation. On the one hand, the myriad divisions it brought are nothing to celebrate. In light of Jesus' last prayer that his followers "may all be one" (John 17), Christian disunity is a tragedy and a scandal. On the other hand, the pope seems to appreciate Luther's reforming zeal, especially his passion for a freer and humbler church.

Like the other reformers, both Protestant and Catholic, Luther took up the humanist battle cry of *ad fontes* – back to the sources! For Luther, that meant going back to the Bible and the early church. If we want reformation and unity today, we must go back to these same sources. It's too bad that Luther himself didn't go farther.

But during the Reformation, there was a group of radicals who did go farther, though hated by both sides. Amid the quincentennial hoopla, they have garnered little attention, but that neglect is unjust. If the Reformation was a battle for the soul of Europe, then they may have been its true winners. Yes, I mean the Anabaptists.

That the Anabaptists won the Reformation is of course a provocative claim, and needs some caveats. Their victory (we'll stick with the chest-thumping language for now) was certainly not in terms of numbers. In the sixteenth century, vicious government persecution – enthusiastically endorsed by Luther, Calvin, and the pope, who agreed on this subject, if little else – nearly wiped out what was a grassroots movement; thousands were executed. Today, Anabaptists, who include Mennonites, the Amish, Hutterites, Church of the Brethren, and the Bruderhof, make up only about 0.1 percent of the 2.2 billion Christians worldwide.

Anabaptism is global and diverse – a surprise to Americans familiar only with its bonnet-and-buggy image. Two-thirds live in Africa, Asia, and Latin America; India, Ethiopia, and the Democratic Republic of the Congo each contain four times as many Anabaptists as does all of Europe.[1] Still, in the great worldwide community of Christians, Anabaptists are a demographic footnote.

Where the Anabaptists win is in the enduring impact of their ideas, once condemned as subversive. In keeping with the Reformers' *ad fontes* credo, these insights were not innovative, but rather a recovery of early Christianity. I'll examine three here: religious liberty, nonviolence, and community. Each of these is crucial to Christianity's future survival, and essential to what a reformed church looks like today.

Religious Freedom

For its first three centuries, the church vigorously affirmed the freedom of the individual conscience. As Tertullian wrote: "It is a fundamental human right, a privilege of nature, that every man should worship according to his own convictions. . . . It is assuredly no part of religion to compel religion – to which free will and not force should lead us."[2]

By the Reformation era, however, Christianity had largely forgotten this. The medieval church, convinced that altar and throne must form an integral whole, handed dissenters over to the state for execution. It wasn't until Vatican II that Catholicism fully embraced religious liberty, as George Weigel

1. Mennonite World Conference, *World Directory*, 2015. mwc-cmm.org/article/world-directory.
2. Tertullian, *To Scapula* 2.

points out (page 45). Luther began his reform with a courageous stand for freedom of conscience – "Here I stand, I can do no other" – but was soon urging Christian princes to enforce his own version of orthodoxy, with the sword if necessary. In Geneva, Calvin had the polymath scholar Michael Servetus burned alive for questioning the Trinity.

Anabaptists, by contrast, abhorred coercion in matters of faith. In the words of an early Anabaptist teaching: "We do not put pressure on anyone who does not join [the church] of his own free will. We desire to persuade no one with smooth words. It is not a matter of human compulsion from without or within, for God wants voluntary service. Whoever cannot do this with joy and to the delight of his soul should therefore leave it alone."[3]

Anabaptists' signature practice of adult baptism is, among other things, a celebration of religious freedom: only those should be baptized who freely choose the Christian way on the basis of personal conviction, something infants are not capable of. Religious liberty is often regarded as something forced onto a reluctant Christianity by the Enlightenment and modern democracy. In reality, as the Anabaptists saw, the individual's free choice lies at the heart of the gospel.

Nonviolence

The early church prohibited all killing, whether in war, self-defense, abortion, or euthanasia, based on Jesus' words in the Sermon on the Mount and his own example of nonresistance.[4] As with religious liberty, the church abandoned this teaching after Christianity became the official religion of the Roman Empire. Before this, church orders such as the *Apostolic Tradition* had prohibited Christians from enlisting as soldiers; just a few generations later, all soldiers were required to be Christian. The fruits of this shift have been bitter; mass killings, from the Crusades to the Native American genocides, have been perpetrated in Christ's name.

In 1527, the Anabaptist leader Michael Sattler was charged in his heresy trial with abetting the Islamic invasion of Europe by refusing to fight – an accusation that sounds eerily contemporary. Sattler replied: "If the Turks should come, we ought not to resist them. For it is written, 'Thou shalt not kill.' We must not defend ourselves against the Turks and others of our persecutors, but are to beseech God with earnest prayer to repel and resist them."[5]

As a result of these words, Sattler died at the stake. His was not the last death for the sake of nonviolence. In the United States one hundred years ago this November, two young Hutterites who refused to don a military uniform died as a result of months of abuse in the Alcatraz prison.[6] In our day, nonviolent Anabaptists in Nigeria have been the primary victims of Boko Haram terrorists.[7]

In recent decades, Catholics and Protestants have been rediscovering their nonviolent heritage, as represented by Christian pacifists such as Martin Luther King Jr. and Dorothy Day.

> **If the Reformation was a battle for the soul of Europe, then the Anabaptists may have been its true winners.**

3. Hutterian baptismal instruction, ca. 1580, in *Taufbüchlein*, ed. Johannes Waldner (ca. 1800).
4. See Ron Sider, *The Early Church on Killing* (Baker, 2012).
5. Michael Sattler, "Trial," in George H. Williams and A. M. Mergal, *Spiritual and Anabaptist Writers* (Westminster, 1957), 141.
6. Duane Stoltzfus, "The Martyrs of Alcatraz," *Plough* No. 1, Summer 2014.
7. Peggy Gish, "Learning to Love Boko Haram," *Plough* No. 6, Autumn 2015.

Almost all major churches support the right to conscientious objection, and popes and theologians have grown wary of justifying warfare in practice, even if Just War theory remains on the books. As Pope John XXIII wrote in *Pacem in Terris*, "It is contrary to reason to hold that war is any longer a suitable way to restore violated rights."

Community

Early Christianity was not just a Sunday religion or a private affair. It meant belonging to the fellowship of disciples, whose way of life was countercultural to that of the surrounding pagan society. In practical terms, this meant participating in an "intense, mutual, disciplined community life," in Rowan Williams's words (page 22). Membership in the church involved accountability, daily rhythms of worship, and economic sharing.[8]

To both Catholics and Protestants of the Reformation era, for whom church and society almost completely overlapped, the suggestion that the church should be a countercultural community would have seemed nonsensical. Christianity *was* the culture, or at least very nearly. True, radical movements of renewal had repeatedly sprung up: monastics such as the Benedictines, itinerants such as the Franciscans, and lay movements such as the Beguines and Beghards. Yet unlike the early church, these movements were for celibates – a special calling for a spiritual vanguard, not the normal way of being Christian. Luther's abolition of the monastic orders eliminated even this remnant of early Christian community from Protestant territories.

To the Anabaptists, the Apostolic Creed's fellowship of believers was to be a practical everyday reality, not just a spiritual one. They drew inspiration from the first church in Jerusalem (Acts 2 and 4). As the Anabaptist Bernhard Rothmann wrote in 1534, "The living communion of saints has been restored, which provides the basis of community of goods among us. . . . Everything which has served the purposes of self-seeking and private property, such as buying and selling, working for money, taking interest and practicing usury . . . or eating and drinking the sweat of the poor, and indeed everything which offends against love – all such things are abolished among us by the power of love and community."[9]

Today, Christians of all traditions are realizing that we are again called, in the words of Rabbi Lord Jonathan Sacks, to form a creative minority. This means building "thick" communities in which disciples can be formed and the faith passed on to the next generation. Recent books by writers as diverse as Russell Moore, Rod Dreher, and Archbishop Charles Chaput are helping to point out the way. Pastors such as Jin Kim and Claudio Oliver are exploring how to practice communal Christianity in different contexts (pages 32 and 38). The Anabaptists' example proves that this is no mere pipe dream, but an actual possibility . . . and a necessity?

Certainly, the picture is incomplete unless we acknowledge Anabaptism's weaknesses over the last five centuries, including a tendency to legalism and a bewildering number of schisms. Yet isn't it remarkable that this ragtag movement, made up primarily of artisans and farmers, got so much right that Europe's greatest minds got wrong? In the Anabaptists' communities, the spirit of early Christianity came alive because they went *ad fontes* – back to the sources – and *ad fontem* – back to the Source. We should all do the same. ➤

8. See Alan Kreider, *The Patient Ferment of the Early Church* (Baker, 2016).

9. Bernhard Rothmann, "Restitution," in Lowell H. Zuck, *Christianity and Revolution* (Temple, 1975), 100.

Remembering Johann Christoph Arnold

On J. Heinrich Arnold II's "Not a Saint, but a Prophet: Remembering My Father," Summer 2017:

What an excellent article by a son about his dear father, Johann Christoph Arnold, certainly a saint in my book. A line that struck me most in this very interesting article was that his father "listened more than he spoke," something sorely missing in today's world – be it among politicians or ordinary mortals.

Mervyn Maciel, Surrey, UK

J. Heinrich II's words about his father are wonderful. What I admire most is his capacity to love. I am so very grateful to have been able to at least read and know Johann Christoph, his father, and his grandfather, if only vicariously. It's a very small world when we are able to love.

Luke Looschen, Rosharon, TX

Joe Strummer – Really?

On Jason Landsel's "Forerunners" column: It has been difficult to understand the purpose of the "Forerunners" section. Is it to hold up certain people as heroes, role models, men and women of faith whose lives we would like to emulate in some way? Why then does it include people like Joe Strummer or Muhammad Ali? I have no doubt that there are things we could learn from both men, but at the same time there were major areas in both of their lives that seriously distract from the message of discipleship to Jesus Christ that I think you wish to present. In lifting these men up as heroes and pointing out their good points without ever a note of caution, the message one receives is that it really doesn't matter that much how I live my life overall, as long as I have some good cause or do some good things. In fact, it really doesn't even matter if I'm a Christian or not. Is that truly the message you wish to present?

Don't misunderstand me: I think there is a place for giving credit to men and women who have been a good example in some way but whose lives in general we may not approve of. However, to feature such people in a special place in your magazine, giving the impression that they are heroes of the faith, is a different matter. Is there really a shortage of heroes of the faith whose lives in general can be upheld as a consistent witness to the one true God and our Lord and Savior Jesus Christ?

Joshua Geiser, Caneyville, KY

Jason Landsel replies: I'll respond with a story. Growing up in a pacifist Christian community, I subconsciously carried an aloofness toward members of the military: I viewed them, in fact, as sinners. But my moralism was challenged when I befriended Larry Mason, a Vietnam veteran whom I featured in an earlier column. Larry and I were close friends for many years, and when my wife and I married, he became part of our family. Together we spent weekends volunteering at the local National Guard base and VFW post. There I met some of the most committed and caring people I've ever encountered. My friend, who was now "Grandpa Larry" to my kids, never lost the many rough edges to his personality, but in his daily life I saw one of the greatest personal faiths lived out.

In "Forerunners," I'd occasionally like to take the reader on a similar journey. I could cherry-pick the top ten saints of all time, but that would be too predictable. Since all human beings are made in the image of God, there must be an element of the divine at work in any human being who seeks, however imperfectly, to do good. Larry taught me to have reverence for this divine spark. Ultimately, I believe, that's the example given us by Jesus himself, who praised the faith of a Gentile centurion, doubtless much to the exasperation of the pious. In that light, even a Muslim heavyweight champion or an English punk rocker can be counted among those – to use Geiser's words – "whose lives we would like to emulate in some way."

Albert Anker, *Elderly Woman Reading the Bible*

Read more reader responses at plough.com/letters. *We welcome letters to the editor. Letters and web comments may be edited for length and clarity, and may be published in any medium. Letters should be sent with the writer's name and address to* letters@plough.com.

El Arado Nicaragua photographs courtesy of Jairo Condega Morales

A piñata hangs ready at a school celebration organized by the *Plough* team in the village of San José del Sur on the Nicaraguan island of Ometepe.

El Arado Nicaragua

In the Nicaraguan university town of León, Jairo Condega Morales and his fellow volunteers of El Arado Nicaragua ("*Plough* in Nicaragua") have distributed thousands of Spanish-language *Plough* books for free, in collaborations with the Catholic Church, evangelical congregations, the city school district, and the city teachers' union.

"Nicaragua is the second poorest country in the Western hemisphere, where half the population lives on two dollars or less per day and more than seven out of ten children are born out of wedlock," says Condega Morales. "In this situation, the single most important thing we can do for a child is to encourage her parents to stay together and provide her with a secure two-parent home. Arnold's book *Sex, God, and Marriage* is proving to be a powerful tool to help couples build strong marriages and families." Under the auspices of Bishop César Bosco Vivas Robelo, the El Arado team offers *Sex, God, and Marriage* to engaged couples as part of the diocese's marriage preparation program. In addition, Arnold's *Why Forgive?* now forms part of the conflict resolution curriculum for León's high schools, whose "Rompiendo el ciclo" project was inspired by the Breaking the Cycle forgiveness program that Arnold co-founded with police detective Steven McDonald. *La violencia del amor,* a collection of the writings of Óscar Romero, the martyred archbishop of San Salvador, is another especially popular title.

The El Arado team has also distributed *Plough* titles to the thirty-one Catholic churches on Ometepe, a two-volcano island in Lake Nicaragua with a population of thirty thousand. Reachable from the mainland only by a ninety-minute ferry ride, Ometepe is renowned for its wildlife but economically isolated. An island native, Condega Morales works with Father Miguel Rodriguez, a parish priest, and with the local Association of Indigenous Youth to bring *Plough* books to Ometepe's primary schools and adult education centers. Several Ometepe villages have

built one-room "library" structures to house the books and provide a reading room with two benches.

Since 2015, the Nicaragua team has given out more than sixteen thousand books, each of which is hand-delivered to a selected school or church. The cost of logistics and of printing by a local firm is borne by *Plough.* Anyone who would like to support this work is invited to make a donation to *Plough* marked "Nicaragua." *plough.com/donate*

Donuts for Books

You don't have to go as far as this Utah church to enjoy the benefits of partnering with *Plough,* but we still think it's cool: using proceeds from donuts and ice cream they make and sell, members of Living Water Mennonite Church buy discounted *Plough* books to give away free. Sign up for Plough Partners to receive discounted books, pre-pub review copies, a free quarterly subscription, and more: *plough.com/partners.*

Beethoven in Sing Sing

While performing classical music for inmates at Rikers Island Correctional Facility,

Brooklyn-based violist and composer Nathan Schram noticed how powerfully the music affected his audience. Convinced that the collaborative process of learning and playing instruments could help inmates cope with life in prison and back at home, Schram established Musicambia, an intensive music education program that fosters humane rehabilitation in prisons. Musicambia instructors provide weekly music theory and performance classes at Sing Sing Correctional Facility in Ossining, New York; the program partners with ten other correctional facilities around the world and hopes to expand.

At Musicambia's recent fundraising concert at the DiMenna Center in Manhattan, three graduates of the program performed "Amazing Grace" and "Smoke Gets in Your Eyes" in trumpet, violin, and voice arrangements they had written while inmates at Sing Sing. One audience member wrote, "Practicing music together gave them a sense of community, a realization of the joy and hope you can bring to others through music. Through the notes they played, something of the same heart-to-heart connection came to all of us."

Despite the enthusiastic efforts of program staff, Musicambia currently lacks the resources to expand to other prisons: Sing Sing alone has a waiting list of more than one hundred inmates who hope to participate. Find out how you can help spread change through music at *musicambia.org.* ➤

Top left, Jairo Condega Morales *(left)* and El Arado volunteers deliver each book personally.

Above, Sing Sing inmates practice a classical arrangement for strings.

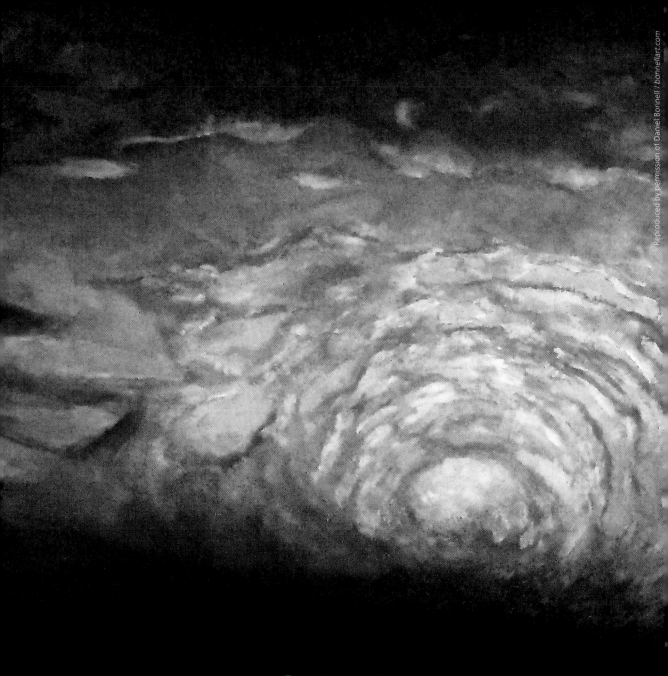

THE **SPIRIT** OF THE

Daniel Bonnell, *The Road to Emmaus,* oil on canvas, 2015

The early church was not perfect, nor can it be blindly imitated, admits Eberhard Arnold in this groundbreaking 1926 essay. And yet: never since in church history has the Spirit been so forcefully at work. Why has the example of the first Christians never ceased to fuel renewal and reform?

EBERHARD ARNOLD

EARLY CHURCH

J ESUS BROUGHT a fresh new message to the world. It is a message that heralds both judgment and rebirth. It announces a totally different social order: the coming reign of God, which will bring to an end the present age ruled by man. Without God we sink down into hollowness and coldness of heart, into stubbornness and self-delusion. In Jesus the Father revealed his love to us, a love that wants to conquer and rule everything that once belonged to it. Jesus calls, urging a divided humankind to sit together at one table, God's table, where there is room for all. He invites all people to a meal of fellowship and fetches his guests from the roadsides and skid rows. The future age comes as God's banquet, God's wedding feast, God's reign of unity. God will be Lord over his creation again, consummating the victory of his spirit of unity and love.

In the Lord's Prayer, Jesus calls on God, our Father, that his primal will should alone prevail on earth, that the future age in which he alone rules should draw near (Matt. 6:10). His being, his name, shall at last be honored because he alone is worthy. Then God will liberate us from all the evil of the present world, from its wickedness and death, from Satan, the evil one now ruling. God grants forgiveness of sin by revealing his power and his love. This saves and protects us in the hour of temptation, the hour of crisis for the whole world. In this way God conquers the earth, with the burden of its historical development and the necessity of daily nourishment.

However, the dark powers of godlessness pervade the world as it is today so strongly that they can be conquered only in the last stronghold of the enemy's might, in death itself. So Jesus calls us to his heroic way of an utterly ignominious death. The catastrophe of the final battle must be provoked, for Satan with all his demonic powers can be driven out in no other way. Jesus' death on the cross is the decisive act. This death makes Jesus the sole leader on the new way that reflects the coming time of God. It makes him the sole captain in the great battle that will consummate God's victory (Heb. 12:1–3).

There is a gulf between these two deadly hostile camps, between the present and the future: between the age we live in and the age to come. Therefore the heroism of Jesus is untimely, hostile in every way to the spirit of the age. For his way subjects every aspect and every condition of today's life to the coming goal of the future. God's time is in the future, yet it has been made known now. Its essence and nature and power became a person in Jesus, became history in him, clearly stated in his words and victoriously fought out in his life and deeds. In this Messiah alone God's future is present.

The new future puts an end to all powers, legal systems, and property laws now in force. The coming kingdom reveals itself even now wherever God's all-powerful love unites people in a life of surrendered brotherhood. Jesus

> IN WHOM ELSE could we, criminals and godless people that we are, be justified except in the Son of God alone? What wonderful exchange, what inscrutable design, what unexpected act of goodness: the injustice of the many was to be covered by the one who is righteous, and the righteousness of the one was to justify the many sinners!
>
> *Letter to Diognetus 9:4–5*

Eberhard Arnold (1883–1935) was a German Protestant theologian, founding editor of Plough, *and with his wife, Emmy Arnold, the founder of the Bruderhof communities.*

proclaimed and brought nothing but God, nothing but his coming rule and order. He founded neither churches nor sects [*weder Kirche noch Sekte*]. His life belonged to greater things. Pointing toward the ultimate goal, he gave the direction. He brought us God's compass, which determines the way by taking its bearings from the pole of the future.

Jesus called people to a practical way of loving brotherhood (Mark 10:28–31). This is the only way in keeping with our expectation of that which is coming. It alone leads us to others; it alone breaks down the barriers erected by the covetous will to possess, because it is determined to give itself to all. The Sermon on the Mount (Matt. 5–7) depicts the liberating power of God's love wherever it rules supreme. When Jesus sent out his disciples and ambassadors, he gave them their work assignment, without which no one can live as he did: in word and deed we are to proclaim the imminence of the kingdom (Matt. 10, Mark 6:7–11, Luke 9:1–6). He gives authority to overcome diseases and demonic powers. To oppose the order of the present world epoch and focus on the task at hand we must abandon all possessions and take to the road. The hallmark of his mission is readiness to become a target for people's hatred in the fierce battle of spirits, and finally, to be killed in action.

The First Followers

After Jesus was killed, the small band of his disciples in Jerusalem proclaimed that though their leader had been shamefully executed, he was indeed still alive and remained their hope and faith as the bringer of the kingdom.[1] The present age, they said, was nearing its end. Humankind was now faced with the greatest turning point ever in its history, and Jesus would appear a second time in glory and authority. God's rule over the whole earth would be ensured.

The powers of this future kingdom could already be seen at work in the early church. People were transformed and made new (Acts 2–4). The strength to die inherent in Jesus' sacrifice led them to accept the way of martyrdom, and more, it assured them of victory over demonic powers of wickedness and disease. He who rose to life through the Spirit had a strength that exploded in an utterly new attitude to life: love to one's brother and love to one's enemy, the divine justice of the coming kingdom. Through this new spirit, property was abolished in the

---

1. The first disciples gave witness to the cross, the resurrection, and the future kingdom, and showed that through love, the power of the Holy Spirit could overcome the power of private property and heal people. The Acts of the Apostles, especially chapters 2–4, describes this decisive manifestation of the church.

early church (Acts 2:42–47; 4:32–37). Material possessions were handed over to the ambassadors for the poor of the church. Through the presence and power of the Spirit and through faith in the Messiah, this band of followers became a brotherhood.

This was their immense task: to challenge the people of Israel in the face of imminent catastrophe, and more, to shake the whole of humankind from its sleep in the face of certain destruction, so that all might prepare for the coming of the kingdom. The poorest people suddenly knew that their new faith was the

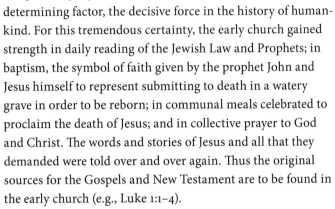

determining factor, the decisive force in the history of humankind. For this tremendous certainty, the early church gained strength in daily reading of the Jewish Law and Prophets; in baptism, the symbol of faith given by the prophet John and Jesus himself to represent submitting to death in a watery grave in order to be reborn; in communal meals celebrated to proclaim the death of Jesus; and in collective prayer to God and Christ. The words and stories of Jesus and all that they demanded were told over and over again. Thus the original sources for the Gospels and New Testament are to be found in the early church (e.g., Luke 1:1–4).

"Lord, come!" – *Maranatha!* – was their age-old cry of faith and infinite longing, preserved in the original Aramaic from this early time of first love. He who was executed and buried is not dead. He draws near as the sovereign living one. The Messiah Jesus has risen from the dead and his kingdom will break in at his second coming! That was the message of his first followers, such as Peter, who led the church at Jerusalem at its founding.

The War between Future and Present

God's new order can break in with all its splendor only after cataclysmic judgment. Death must come before the resurrection of the flesh. The promise of a future millennium is linked to the prophecy of judgment, which will attack the root of the prevailing order (Rev. 19–20). All this springs from the original message passed on by the very first church. There is tension between future and present, God and demons; between selfish, possessive will and the loving, giving will of God; between the present order of the state, which through economic pressures assumes absolute power, and God's coming rule of love and justice. These two antagonistic forces sharply provoke each other. The present world age is doomed; in fact, the promised Messiah has already overpowered its champion and leader! This is an accomplished fact. The early church handed down this superhistorical revolution to the next generation. Jesus rose from the dead; too late did the prince of death realize his power was broken.[2]

2. Ignatius, *Letter to the Ephesians* 19:3.

From the time of the early church and the apostle Paul, the cross remains the one and only proclamation (1 Cor. 2:1–2):[3] Christians shall know only one way, that of being nailed to the cross with Christ. Only dying his death with him leads to resurrection and to the kingdom.[4] No wonder that Celsus, an enemy of the church, was amazed at the centrality of the cross and the resurrection among the Christians.[5] The pagan satirist Lucian was surprised that one who was hung on the cross in Palestine could have introduced this death as a new mystery: dying with him on the cross was the essence of his bequest.[6] The early Christians used to stretch out their hands as a symbol of triumph, imitating the arms extended on the cross.

THIS AGE and the one that is coming are two enemies. This one talks about adultery and corruption and greed and deceit, but that one renounces these things. We cannot, therefore, be friends of both; we must renounce this one in order to experience that one.

Second Letter of Clement 6:3–5

In their certainty of victory, Christians who gathered for the Lord's Supper heard the alarmed question of Satan and death, "Who is he that robs us of our power?" They answered with the exultant shout of victory, "Here is Christ, the crucified!"[7] Proclaiming Christ's death at this meal meant giving substance to his resurrection, allowing it to transform their lives. This transformation proved the decisive fact of Christ's victory, born of power and giving power, consummated in his suffering and dying, in his rising from death and ascent to the throne, and in his second coming. For what Christ has done he does again and again in his church. His victory is perfected. Terrified, the devil must give up his own. The dragon with seven heads is slain. The evil venom is destroyed.[8]

Thus the church sings the praise of him who became man, who suffered, died, and rose again, and overpowered the realm of the underworld when he descended into Hades. He is "the strong," "the mighty," "the immortal."[9] He comes in person to his church, escorted by the hosts of his angel princes. Now the heavens are opened to the believers. They see and hear the choir of singing angels. Christ's coming to the church in the power of the Spirit, here and now, makes his first historical coming and his second, future appearance a certainty. In trembling awe the church experiences her Lord and sovereign as a guest:

3. The same words are used in *Acts of Peter* 37: "The cross of Christ, who is the Word stretched out, the one and only, of whom the Spirit saith: For what else is Christ, but the Word, the sound of God?" See also *Acts of John* 94–95, 98–99.
4. Ignatius, *Letter to the Smyrnaeans* 1–3.
5. Origen, *Against Celsus* VI.34.
6. Lucian, *On the Death of Peregrinus* 11.
7. The Syriac *Testament of Our Lord Jesus Christ* 1:28; the Arabic *Didascalia* (Chapter 39, where it is introduced as *mystagogia Jesu Christi*).
8. *Ode of Solomon* 22.
9. See the Liturgy of James and the Liturgy of Mark. See also the so-called "Clementine Liturgy" in the *Apostolic Constitutions* and the Syriac *Testament of Our Lord.*

"Now he has appeared among us!"[10] Some see him sitting in person at the table to share their meal. Celebrating the Lord's Supper is for them a foretaste of the future wedding feast.

The Holy Spirit has descended upon them, and grace has entered their hearts. Their fellowship is complete and perfect. The powers of God penetrate the gathered church. Gripped by the Spirit, filled with the Spirit, they become one with Christ. Ulysses, tied to the mast of the ship, sailed past the Sirens unscathed. In the same way, only those who become one with the Crucified by being tied, as it were, to his cross, can withstand the lures of this storm-tossed world and the violent passions of this age.[11]

The trials of all the Greek heroes, however, cannot match the intensity of this spiritual battle. By becoming one with the triumphant Christ, early Christian life becomes a soldier's life (Eph. 6:10–18), sure of victory over the greatest enemy of all time in the bitter struggle with the dark powers of this world. Murderous weapons, amulets, and magic spells are of no use in this war. Nor will people look to water, oil, incense, burning lamps, music, or even the symbol of the cross to gain victory over demonic powers, as long as they truly believe in the name of Jesus, the power of his spirit, his life in history, and his super-historical victory. Whenever the believers found unity in their meetings, especially when they celebrated baptism or the Lord's Supper and "love meal," the power of Christ's presence was indisputable: sick bodies were healed, demons were driven out, and sins were forgiven. As people turned away from their past wrongs and were freed from all their weaknesses, they could be certain of resurrection and eternal life.

Baptism as Military Oath

The equality achieved by faith meant that every believer who stepped out of the baptismal bath was considered pure and holy (1 Cor. 6:9–11). The anti-Christian Porphyry was appalled that one single washing should purify those covered with guilt and evil, that a glutton, fornicator, adulterer, drunkard, thief, pederast, poisoner, or anyone vile, wicked, or filthy in other ways should simply be baptized, call upon the name of Christ, and with this be freed so easily, casting off such enormous guilt as lightly as a snake sheds its skin. "All they have to do is to believe and be baptized."[12] About this forgiveness and complete removal of guilt, Justin says: "Only those who have

TRAIN TOGETHER with one another: compete together, run together, suffer together, rest together, get up together, as God's managers, assistants, and servants. Please the one whom you serve as soldiers, from whom you receive your wages. Let none of you be found a deserter. Let your baptism serve as a shield, faith as a helmet, love as a spear, endurance as armor. . . . Be patient, therefore, and gentle with one another, as God is with you.

Ignatius, To Polycarp 6:1–2

---

10. The Armenian Liturgy, the *Apostolic Constitutions* VIII, Clementine Liturgy, after Psalm 118:26.
11. The comparison between those tied to the cross (the Christians united with the Crucified One) and Ulysses appears in very early Christian art and writing.
12. Macarius Magnes, *Apocriticus* IV.19, in Porphyry, *Against the Christians*.

truly ceased to sin shall receive baptism."[13] Whoever is baptized must keep the seal pure and inviolate.[14] Such an incredible practical demand, expecting total change, was possible only by faith in the power of the living Spirit, who descends on the water of baptism and makes it a bath of rebirth, a symbol of new life and purity. . . . The conviction of the first Christians rested on their deep belief in baptism. Through their faith in the Holy Spirit they were the church of believers that could forgive every sin, because in it every sin was overcome. Many came to the Christians, impressed by the possibility of a totally new way of living and looking for a power that would save them from their unworthy lives.[15]

More and more soldiers of the Spirit were sworn to this "military oath" through baptism and the simultaneous confession of faith. This "mystery" bound them to sober service of Christ and the simplicity of his divine works. In the water, believers buried their entire former lives, with all their ties and involvements. Plunged so deeply into the crucified Christ that the water could be likened to his blood, they accepted as their own the victory of the cross and its power to sever all demonic powers. Now they could live in the strength of the Risen One. Each believer broke with the entire status quo and was thereby committed to live and to die for the cause embraced through such a consecration unto death. The new time invaded the old with a company of fighters pledged to die, a triumphal march of truth and power.

> I T IS GOD himself who has brought the human race to holding all things in common, first of all by sharing himself, by sending his Word to all people alike, and by making all things for all. Therefore, everything is common, and the rich should not grasp the greater share. The expression, "I own something, and have more than enough. Why should I not enjoy it?" is not worthy of a man and does not indicate any community feeling. The other expression does, however: "I have something, why should I not share it with those who have need of it?" Such a one is perfect, and fulfills the command: "Thou shalt love thy neighbor as thyself."
>
> *Clement of Alexandria, The Instructor II.13*

Love and Economics

During the first two centuries . . . the movement spread almost exclusively among slaves, freedmen, and artisans. The makeup of the membership was reflected in the value the church put on work (1 Thess. 5:12–13). Everyone was expected to earn his or her living and to produce enough to help others in want. Each had to work, so that his love could help the needs of others. Therefore the church had to discern and procure labor. This obligation shows how fully the

13. Justin, *First Apology* 61.
14. *Second Letter of Clement* 6:9. "What assurance do we have of entering the kingdom of God if we fail to keep our baptism pure and undefiled?"
15. Cyprian, *To Donatus* 3–5.

Christian communities shared their work and goods.[16] Whoever was not willing to do the work he was capable of – whoever was "trading on Christ" – was not tolerated in the communities. "An idler can never be a believer."[17]

The freedom to work voluntarily and the possibility of putting one's capabilities to use were the practical basis for all acts of love and charity. Self-determination in their work gave an entirely voluntary character to all social work done by the early Christians. Hermas gives another indication of the spirit ruling in the church. He writes that the wealthy can be fitted into the building of the church only after they strip themselves of their wealth for the sake of their poorer brothers and sisters.[18] Wealth was regarded as deadly to the owner and had to be made serviceable to the public by being given away. The early Christians taught that just as in nature – the origin and destiny of creation – the light, air, and soil belong to all, so too material goods should be the common property of all.

The practice of surrendering everything in love was the hallmark of the Christians. When this declined, it was seen as a loss of the spirit of Christ (John 13:35). Urged by this love, many even sold themselves into slavery or went to debtors' prison for the sake of others. Nothing was too costly for the Christians when the common interest of their brotherhood was at stake; they developed an incredible activity in the works of love.[19]

In fact, everything the church owned at that time belonged to the poor. The affairs of the poor were the affairs of the church; every gathering served to support bereft women and children, the sick, and the destitute.[20] The basic feature of the movement, a spirit of boundless giving, was more essential than the resulting communal life and the rejection of private property. In the early church the spontaneity of genuine love merged private property into a "communism of love." This same urge of love later made Christian women of rank give away their property and become beggars. The pagans deplored the fact that instead of commanding respect by means of their wealth, these women became truly pitiful creatures, knocking at doors of houses much less respected than their own had

> BE EAGER, THEN, in coming together as often as possible for God's Meal of Thanksgiving and for his praises, for if you meet frequently, Satan's powers are broken; what he threatens you with is dashed to pieces on the unity of your faith. There is nothing better than the peace by which all warfare waged by heavenly and earthly powers is abolished.
>
> *Ignatius, Letter to the Ephesians 13:1–2*

16. *Didache* 12:2–5.
17. 2 Thess. 3:6–15. See *Didascalia* 8.
18. Hermas, *The Shepherd* 14:5–6, 17:2–5.
19. The pagan Lucian, in *The Death of Peregrinus* 13, describes how the Christians rallied to support one of their number when he was imprisoned.
20. See Justin, *First Apology* 67.

been.[21] To help others, the Christians took the hardest privations upon themselves (Heb. 10:32–34). Nor did they limit their works of love to fellow believers.[22] Even Emperor Julian had to admit that "the godless Galileans feed our poor in addition to their own."[23]

According to Christians, the private ownership of property sprang from the primordial sin of humankind: it was the result of covetous will. However necessary property might be for life in the present demonic epoch, the Christian could not cling to it. The private larder or storeroom had to be put at the disposal of guests and wanderers just as much as the common treasury.[24] Nor could anybody evade the obligation to extend hospitality. In this way each congregation reached out far beyond its own community.

But in other ways too, the communities helped their brothers and sisters in different places. In very early times the church at Rome enjoyed high esteem in all Christian circles because it "presided in works of love."[25] The rich capital city was able to send help in all directions, whereas the poorer Jerusalem had to accept support from other churches in order to meet the needs of the crowds of pilgrims that thronged its streets. Within its own city, the relatively small church at Rome gave regular support to fifteen hundred distressed persons in the year AD 250.[26] . . . Christians spent more money in the streets than the followers of other religions spent in their temples. Working for the destitute was a distinguishing mark of the first Christians.

The New Humanity

The rank afforded by property and profession is incompatible with such fellowship and simplicity, and repugnant to it. For that reason alone, the early Christians had an aversion to any high judicial position or commission in the army.[27] They found it impossible to take responsibility for any penalty or imprisonment, any disfranchisement, any judgment over life or death, or the execution of any death sentence pronounced by martial or criminal courts.

> WE OURSELVES WERE well conversant with war, murder, and everything evil, but all of us throughout the whole wide earth have traded in our weapons of war. We have exchanged our swords for plowshares, our spears for farm tools. Now we cultivate the fear of God, justice, kindness to all, faith, and the expectation of the future given to us by the Father himself through the Crucified One.
>
> *Justin, Dialogue with Trypho 110:3*

21. Macarius Magnes, *Apocriticus* III.5, Porphyry Fragment 58.
22. See *Didascalia* XIX: "That it is a duty to take care of those who for the name of Christ suffer affliction as martyrs."
23. Julian, *To Arsacius.*
24. Tertullian, *To His Wife* II.4.
25. Ignatius, *Letter to the Romans,* Salutation.
26. Bishop Cornelius in Eusebius, *Church History* VI.43.
27. One could agree to a Christian's right to hold a high office in which he was empowered to adjudicate over the civic rights of a person only if he did not condemn or penalize anyone, or cause anyone to be put into chains, thrown into prison, or tortured (Tertullian, *On Idolatry* 17).

Other trades and professions were out of the question because they were connected with idolatry or immorality. Christians, therefore, had to be prepared to give up their occupations. The resulting unemployment and threat of hunger would be no more frightening than violent death by martyrdom.[28]

Underpinning these practical consequences was unity of word and deed. A pattern of daily life emerged that was consistent with the message that the Christians proclaimed. Most astounding to the outside observer was the extent to which poverty was overcome in the vicinity of the communities, through voluntary works of love. It had nothing to do with the more or less compulsory social welfare of the state.

Chastity before marriage, absolute faithfulness in marriage, and strict monogamy were equally tangible changes. In the beginning this was expressed most clearly in the demand that brothers in responsible positions should have only one wife (1 Tim. 3:2). The foundation for Christian marriage was purely religious: marriage was seen as a symbol of the relationship of the one God with his one people, the one Christ with his one church.

From then on, a completely different humanity was in the making. This shows itself most clearly in the religious foundation of the family, which is the starting point of every society and fellowship, and in the movement toward a "communism of love," which is the predominant tendency of all creation. The new people, called out and set apart by God, are deeply linked to the coming revolution and renewal of the whole moral and social order. It is a question of the most powerful affirmation of the earth and humankind. Through their Creator and his miraculous power, the believers expect the perfection of social and moral conditions. This is the most positive attitude imaginable: they expect God's perfect love to become manifest for all people, comprehensively and universally, answering their physical needs as well as the need of their souls.

> WHEN THE BLESSED evangelist John, the apostle, had lived in Ephesus into his extreme old age and could hardly be carried to the meetings of the church by the disciples, and when in speaking he could no longer put together many words, he would not say anything else in the meetings but this: "Little children, love one another!" When at last the disciples and brothers present got tired of hearing the same thing again and again, they said, "Master, why do you keep saying the same thing?" John replied with a saying worthy of him: "Because it is the Lord's command, and it is enough if it is really done."
>
> *Jerome, Commentary on Galatians 6:10*

28. Tertullian, *On Idolatry* 12: "Faith does not fear hunger."

And What Now?

Despite all later deviations from the early time of revelation, no church or sect in Christendom has ever completely forgotten that love remains the supreme sacrament of faith, the treasure of the Christian faith.[29] Bearing in mind the radicalism of all sects, the narrowness of all monastic exercises in devotion, and the vast responsibilities of the organized churches, Irenaeus was right in saying, "It remains, as in the time now past, that the greatest is the free gift of brotherly love, which is more glorious than knowledge, more marvelous than prophecy, and more sublime than all other gifts of grace."[30]

In the fire of first love, in the many signs of God at work, the rich, primitive force of the early Christian spirit continues to speak to us. All the moments of power and truth characteristic of New Testament Christianity can be sensed here, as well as the roots of developments that later led to the organized churches. A clearly defined way of life and faith arises from the manifestation of God in early Christian times. It continues to be a living force today in spite of rigidity in later centuries. Because it comes from the wellspring of living truth, this way can never be achieved merely through external imitation.

There is only one criterion for this way: the direct, spontaneous testimony which the Spirit himself brings from God and from Christ. It is the witness of faith, speaking to us from apostolic and prophetic experience. The original witness of the church must lead us all, placed as we are today in very different camps, into the unity and purity of the clear light. The period of original revelation must be the point of departure for any dialogue between the many churches, sects, and movements of our own day. The awakening and uniting of all who truly desire to follow Christ, so much needed today, will be given at the source, and nowhere else. ⟞

WHO CAN DESCRIBE the bond of God's love? Who is able to explain the majesty of its beauty? The height to which love leads is indescribable. Love unites us with God; love covers a multitude of sins; love endures all things, is patient in all things. There is nothing coarse, nothing arrogant in love. Love knows nothing of schisms, love leads no rebellions, love does everything in harmony. In love all the elect of God were made perfect; without love nothing is pleasing to God.

First Clement 49:2–5

29. Cf. Tertullian, *On the Prescription of Heretics* 20.
30. Irenaeus, *Against Heresies* IV.33:1, 8.

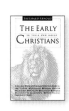

This article is excerpted from Arnold's book The Early Christians: In Their Own Words *(Plough, 1997). Get the free ebook at* plough.com/earlychristians.

The Two Ways

ROWAN WILLIAMS

THERE ARE

one of death

THE WAY
OF DEATH

BVT THE WAY OF DEATH IS
THIS IT IS EVIL AND COM
PLETELY CVRSED MVR
DERS ADVLTRIES LVSTS
SEXVAL IMMORALITIES
THEFTS IDOLATRIES MA
GIC ARTS SORCERIES R
OBBERIES FALSE TESTIM
ONIES HYPOCRICIES DV
PLICITY DECEIT PRIDE
MALICE STVBBORNNE

THE WAY OF LIFE

Now this is the way of life: first you shall love God who made you. Second, you shall love your neighbor as yourself; but whatever you do not wish to happen to you, do not do to another.

TWO WAYS

and there is a great difference between these two ways

To whom do we give our loyalty? The early Christians teach us that the choice changes everything.

The Two Ways

ROWAN WILLIAMS

Most of the writings that survive from the first three centuries of Christianity are what one twentieth-century philosopher called "death-cell philosophy"; that is, they represent the kind of thinking that is done under extreme pressure, when what you say or think has a genuine life-or-death importance. Gregory Dix, an Anglican monk writing eighty or so years ago about the worship of the early church, imagined what it would be like to attend the Lord's Supper in second-century Rome by recreating the experience in terms of twentieth-century London. He takes the descriptions of worship from texts like the so-called "Teaching of the Twelve Apostles," the *Didache,* probably the most ancient account of worship outside the New Testament, and the *Apostolic Tradition* from the third century, and translates them into the landscape of modern England. A grocer from the unfashionable suburbs slips through the back door of a wealthy brother's house in Kensington at the crack of dawn to share in the breaking of bread in the drawing room – a brief, quiet event, overshadowed by the knowledge that if they would be discovered they would face at least penal servitude for life, and very likely worse. Any Christian in this period knew that, even if things were relatively peaceful, it was always possible that a suspicious government would crack down. Dix describes how the "deacons," the ministers who looked after the doors, were charged with scrutinizing everyone who came in very carefully; you'd need to know who your companions were if your life depended on them.

The suspicions were well founded in one sense. If you look at the eyewitness accounts of martyrdom in these early centuries – documents like the wonderful record of the martyrs of Scilli in North Africa in AD 180 – you can see what the real issue was. These Christians, most of them probably domestic slaves, had to explain to the magistrate that they were quite happy to pray for the imperial state, and even to pay taxes, but that they could not grant the state their absolute allegiance. They had another loyalty – which did not mean that they wished to overthrow the administration, but that they would not comply with the

> **To speak of Jesus as "Lord of Lords" was to say that his decisions could not be overridden by anyone.**

Rowan Williams was the Archbishop of Canterbury from 2002 to 2012. A theologian and poet, he is master of Magdalen College in Cambridge and chancellor of the University of South Wales.

state's demands in certain respects. They would not worship the emperor, and, as we know from some other texts, refused to serve in the Roman army. They asked from the state what had been very reluctantly conceded to the Jews as an ethnic group – exemption from the religious requirements of the empire. What made their demand new and shocking was that it was not made on the basis of ethnic identity, but on the bare fact of conviction and conscience. For the first time in human history, individuals claimed the liberty to define the limits of their political loyalty, and to test that loyalty by spiritual and ethical standards.

That is why the early Christian movement was so threatening – and so simply baffling – to the Roman authorities. It was not revolutionary in the sense that it was trying to change the government. Its challenge was more serious: it was the claim to hold any and every government to account, to test its integrity, and to give and withhold compliance accordingly. But it would be wrong to think of this, as we are tempted to do in our era, in terms of individual conscience. It was about the right of a community to set its own standards and to form its members in the light of what had been given to them by an authority higher than the empire.

The early Christians believed that if Jesus of Nazareth was "Lord," no one else could be lord over him, and therefore no one could overrule his authority. We use the word "Lord" these days mostly in a rather unthinking religious context, as a sort of devotional flourish; for a Roman, it meant the person who made the decisions you had to abide by, from the master of a slave in the household to the emperor himself. To speak of Jesus as "King of Kings and Lord of Lords" was to say that his decisions could not be overridden by anyone. You might have to disobey a "lord" in our society in order to obey the one true Master of all – the one who used no violence in enforcing his decisions but was all the more unanswerable an authority because of that. He alone needed no reinforcement, no temporal power, to overcome external threats or rivals.

E arly Christianity was on the one hand a deeply political community, posing a very specific challenge to the state by saying that the state was a provisional reality – deserving of respect and routine compliance in the ordinary affairs of social life, but having no ultimate claim. On the other hand, it was a movement fascinated by the intellectual implications of what this meant. Because if Jesus is "Lord," and if God needs no force to defend his authority against rivals, then Jesus' "policy" is God's, and Jesus shares without qualification the wisdom and self-sufficiency of God. As early as the beginning of the second century we find the martyred bishop Ignatius from Antioch calling Jesus "God"; Jesus needed no defense against rivals, and so was free to take on himself the burden of human suffering without being crushed or destroyed by it. And because of his own freedom in the face of appalling suffering, he could make it possible for his disciples to face their own suffering with the same resolution and steadiness. What Ignatius called "the passion of my God" was a gift to believers

From the DIDACHE

There are two ways, one of life and one of death, and there is a great difference between these two ways.

The Way of Life

Now this is the way of life: First, you shall love God, who made you. Second, you shall love your neighbor as yourself; but whatever you do not wish to happen to you, do not do to another. The teaching of these words is this: Bless those who curse you, and pray for your enemies, and fast for those who persecute you. For what credit is it if you love those who love you? Do not even the Gentiles do the same? But you must love those who hate you, and you will not have an enemy. Abstain from fleshly and bodily cravings. If someone gives you a blow on your right cheek, turn to him the other as well and you will be perfect. If someone forces you to go one mile, go with him two miles; if someone takes your cloak, give him your tunic also; if someone takes from you what belongs to you, do not demand it back, for you cannot do so.

Give to everyone who asks you, and do not demand it back, for the Father wants something from his own gifts to be given to everyone. Blessed is the one who gives according to the command, for such a person is innocent. Woe to the one who receives: if, on the one hand, someone who is in need receives, this person is innocent, but the one who does not have need will have to explain why and for what purpose he received, and upon being imprisoned will be interrogated about what he has done, and will not be released from there until he has repaid every last cent. But it has also been said concerning this: "Let your gift sweat in your hands until you know to whom to give it."

The second commandment of the teaching is: You shall not murder; you shall not commit adultery; you shall not corrupt children; you shall not be sexually immoral; you shall not steal; you shall not practice magic; you shall not engage in sorcery; you shall not abort a child or commit infanticide. You shall not covet your neighbor's possessions; you shall confronting those terrible risks that Gregory Dix brought alive so vividly in his study of early worshiping life.

The theology of the early centuries thus comes very directly out of this one great central conviction about political authority: if Jesus is Lord, no one else ultimately is, and so those who belong with Jesus, who share his life through the common life of the worshiping community, have a solidarity and a loyalty that goes beyond the chance identity of national or political life. The first claim on their loyalty is to live out the life of Jesus, which is also the life of God – a life that needs no defense and so has no place for violence and coercion. God, says Clement of Alexandria in the late second century, shows his love supremely in the fact that he loves people who have no "natural" claim on him.

not commit perjury; you shall not give false testimony; you shall not speak evil; you shall not hold a grudge. . . . You shall not hate anyone; instead you shall reprove some, and pray for some, and some you shall love more than your own life.

The Way of Death

But the way of death is this: First of all, it is evil and completely cursed; murders, adulteries, lusts, sexual immoralities, thefts, idolatries, magic arts, sorceries, robberies, false testi-monies, hypocrisies, duplicity, deceit, pride, malice, stubbornness, greed, abusive language, jealousy, audacity, arrogance, boast-fulness. It is the way of persecutors of good people, of those who hate truth, love a lie . . . have no mercy for the poor, do not work on behalf of the oppressed, do not know the one who made them, are murderers of children, corrupters of God's creation, who turn away from someone in need, who oppress the afflicted, are advocates of the wealthy, lawless

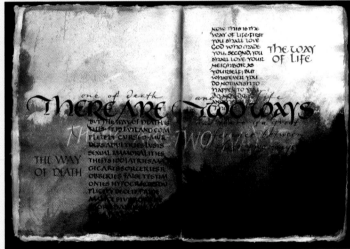

judges of the poor, utterly sinful. May you be delivered, children, from all these things!

Daily Discipleship

See that no one leads you astray from this way of the teaching, for such a person teaches you without regard for God. For if you are able to bear the whole yoke of the Lord, you will be perfect. But if you are not able, then do what you can. ➤

Randall M. Hasson, *The Two Ways*, calligraphy

The Didache *(ca. AD 60–110) is an anonymous teaching for baptismal preparation from an early church community, possibly in Syria. From* Didache *1, 2, 5, and 6 in* The Apostolic Fathers, *ed. Michael Holmes (Baker, 2007).*

Humans love largely because of fellow-feeling, but God's love is such that it never depends on having something in common. The creator has in one sense nothing in common with his creation – how could he? But he is completely free to exercise his essential being, which is love, wherever he wills. And this teaches us that we too must learn to love beyond the boundaries of common interest and natural sympathy and, like God, love those who don't seem to have anything in common with us.

Like God, we must love those who don't seem to have anything in common with us.

This is one of the paradoxes of early Christian thought. It's really deeply rooted in intense, mutual, disciplined community life, but at the same time insists on universal compassion and universal sympathy. The theology of the early church was not an eccentric diversion from the real business of mutual love and generous service. The doctrines of God's eternity and unchangeable consistency, the doctrine of Jesus' full participation in the divine life, ultimately the doctrine that Christians came to call the divine Trinity, and much more, derive directly from saying that Jesus is truly the supreme authority and that he exhibits exactly the same liberty to love indiscriminately as does God himself. Jesus is the earthly face of an eternal love between Father, Son, and Spirit. And when the early theologians write, as they often do, about how Christians are given a share in the divine life or the divine nature – language that can sound a bit shocking to modern believers – what they mean is simply that being in the body of Christ, in the community of baptized believers, gives us the freedom to love God the Father as Jesus loves him, through the gift of the Holy Spirit, and so too to love the world with the unquestioning generosity of God, never restricting ourselves to loving those who are familiar to us and are like us.

Writers on the life of prayer in this period – above all, the great Origen of Alexandria, who taught and wrote in the first half of the third century – associated Christian identity with freedom, the freedom to call God "Father" and Jesus "Lord," as Origen puts it; which is also, for him, a freedom from what he calls (confusingly to our ears) "passion." This doesn't mean that Christians should have no emotions; but that they should be free from reactive, unthinking feelings that dictate their response to people and things. Our response to the world around us must be rooted in a renewal of our minds, seeing through superficial differences to recognize God's presence and purpose in all persons and things.

And for all these great figures, there were blindingly obvious practical implications – to treat each other with forgiveness and respect, to address poverty and suffering, and to step back from the institutions of the state, especially the army. None of this was fully encoded in rules, but the church expected people to be able to draw the obvious conclusions from the simple starting point of living under a new authority. We know that there were Christian soldiers in those centuries, but we know too that the community in general never settled happily with the idea that Christians should bear arms. Origen is one of the many who could not be reconciled to that idea. And even when things were beginning to change drastically in the fourth century, with a Christian emperor who sounded increasingly like his non-Christian predecessors, there were figures like Martin of Tours in France who discovered, when they converted, that they couldn't carry on as soldiers. Even the formidable Augustine of Hippo at the beginning of the fifth century – famous as the man who first outlined the conditions for a "just war" – is crystal clear that, while he thinks Christians may take part in defensive war to protect the weak, we should never try to defend the gospel by war. It's a pity that this side of Augustine's thought was largely overlooked by people eager to make him an ally of just those imperial military myths that he was so regularly scathing about.

We have to admit that, by the fifth century, the church *was* looking different. Having become legal at the beginning of the fourth century, it steadily became more and more involved with the power of the state and was seen as giving legitimacy to the emperor. Those who argued for this were neither wicked nor hypnotized by power and influence (though no doubt some had their temptations). They thought that divine providence had at last put an end to their cruel sufferings and provided them with an ally in the Christian emperor. Augustine is one of those who disagreed strongly with this, but not many took up his approach. For most, it was easier to believe that God had brought human history nearer its fulfillment by converting the power of the state. And it was when all this was going on that some serious Christians started moving away from cities and towns to become monks in the deserts of Egypt and Syria – so that they could reconstruct the life of the first believers in Jerusalem, sharing their property and living in simplicity. For many centuries, indeed, the life of the monks was described as the "apostolic" life. And originally it was a life for laypeople, not clergy; those who became monks were as eager to escape from the hierarchy of the church as from the hierarchy

of the state. In the sermons and stories that were developed in this setting, we find the same themes that appear in earlier writing: the common life of Christians must display the characteristics of the life of the Lord, in unquestioning compassion and mercy, in generosity and simplicity, and in refusing to defend oneself or compare oneself with others.

In this period, the great central theme of Christian existence was how to live in such a way that it was clear where one's loyalty lay – because this was the best way of witnessing to a God whose eternal life was utterly free from competition and conflict. The experience of a new way of living in community prompted theological questioning; the theological clarifications reinforced and deepened the sense of the priorities and imperatives for the community. One of the lasting legacies of the early church, then, is the recognition that doctrine, prayer, and ethics don't exist in tidy separate compartments: each one shapes the others. And in the church in any age, we should not be surprised if we become hazy about our doctrine at a time when we are less clear about our priorities as a community, or if we become

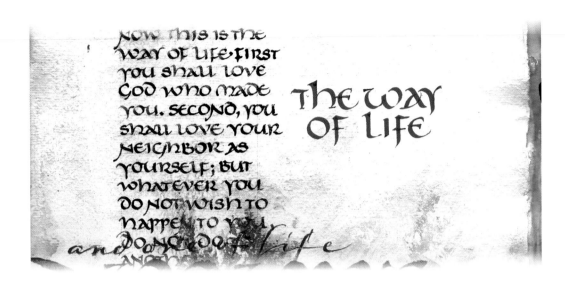

NOW THIS IS THE
WAY OF LIFE. FIRST
YOU SHALL LOVE
GOD WHO MADE
YOU. SECOND, YOU
SHALL LOVE YOUR
NEIGHBOR AS
YOURSELF; BUT
WHATEVER YOU
DO NOT WISH TO
HAPPEN TO YOU

THE WAY OF LIFE

less passionate about service, forgiveness, and peace when we have stopped thinking clearly about the true and eternal character of God.

We need communities of believers trying to live out Christ's radical imperatives.

We don't have to be uncritical of the Christians in that early period. But what they offer us is a clear message about how Christian identity is always a claim to a "citizenship" that is deeper and more universal than any human society can provide. Christians are always going to be living at an angle to the mainstream – not claiming a glib moral superiority, yet insisting that they "march to a different drum" since they recognize final and unsurpassable authority in the living and dying of Jesus of Nazareth. He, they insisted, is the only one who has the right and the liberty to tell us what is real and true in the universe. This does not mean that the church is locked in a violent contest with state or society, that it is struggling for supremacy. If Christ is who we believe him to be, there is never any need for struggle; nothing will make him less real or

true. Insofar as there is a struggle, it is against our own willingness to let other authorities overrule Christ. In the early church, that was a life-and-death matter – and it still is for Christians in some parts of the world today.

For most of us the consequences are less dramatic, but the challenge is still there. Our faith is still a "death-cell philosophy," certainly in a world that confuses "life" with victory, prosperity, or security at the expense of others. We know better what life really is – what must be let go of in order for it to flourish, what astonishing gifts are opened up for those who find the courage to step beyond what is conventionally and religiously taken for granted. And if the struggle is hard – as it is, even if we are not threatened with martyrdom – there is all the more need for communities of believers trying to live out the radical imperatives: communities of monastic discipline in the old way, new communities focused on peace and the disciplines of nonviolence. We can't do any of this as isolated individuals with an interior piety. We need the concrete reality of Christ's corporate Body, nourished by his Supper. ➤

Parable

Here in the suburbs we are annoyed
when the neighbors decide to raise
chickens, build a coop and rise each
day to crows and the promise of eggs.

We pluck feathers from our petunias
and our pools, listen to rasping cackles
as we mow, glance to the sky to plead
for justice and when the hawks fly low.

Only when someone forgets one night
to cinch the latch on the outside fence
can we let our indignation go. Now we
gather our sorrows like the neighbors'

children, who find some way to pick up
the bodies and the bones – feathers from
our yards, too – and accept the old ways
of foxes or coyotes, holding no judgment.

MARY M. BROWN

*Mary M. Brown taught literature and creative writing
at Indiana Wesleyan for many years, and now lives in
Anderson, Indiana.*

Artwork: Olivia Clifton-Bligh, *Red-Breasted Old English
Game Cock,* hand-burnished illuminated linocut print

JIN S. KIM

TIME FOR A NEW

Stirrings
of a Local
Church

Reformation

ON OCTOBER 31, 1517, an Augustinian monk named Martin Luther ignited a movement in the Western church that would lead to the Protestant Reformation. It was a bold response that captured the people's yearning for comprehensive reform of a church that seemed to have lost its moorings. In modern times it has become apparent to more and more Christians that the church seems to be obsessed with its own institutional survival, which is akin to a dog chasing its own tail. What kind of reformation do we need today for the church to remember its identity and pursue its mission?

Every few months at Church of All Nations (CAN), we offer a class for visitors who want to become members of our congregation, and by extension, of the church catholic. In the class we discuss discipleship, membership, and the theological concepts at the core of our community. But the majority of class time is devoted to a two-thousand-year overview of the Christian story. Why do we spend so much time discussing history? We see no other way to know who we are as a church, and where we are going, apart from knowing how we got here.

It doesn't take long for our new member candidates to see that our congregation, though part of the mainline Presbyterian family, draws its inspiration from the radical reformers persecuted as "Anabaptists" by Roman Catholics, Lutherans, and Calvinists. The Anabaptists' clear identification of church–state collusion as idolatry made them a threat to both the Catholic Church and the fledgling Protestant movement. At CAN, our commitment to costly discipleship doesn't come from Reformed catechisms and creeds, but from the way that the Confessing Church emerged to challenge Nazi rule in Germany, and the daring witness of Christians like Dietrich Bonhoeffer – their courage, "real world" theology, and pastoral insights.

Today, we are seeing growing impatience with the institutional church's accommodation to temporal power. Younger generations, no longer willing to give the church the benefit of the doubt, are driving the mass exodus out of the Western church, which they see as a primary source of pain and abuse in the world. But for those who have not given up on the church as a vessel of God's grace and transformation, the contours of a new reformation are beginning to surface.

Our congregation, for instance, is trying to root itself in the anti-imperial gospel community that Jesus inaugurated in Galilee. We hope to be heirs of an unbroken tradition of radical faithfulness to the God of Israel. Though the church has given in to the temptations of empire throughout her history, we are encouraged by the long and continuous witness of uncompromising faithfulness to Jesus as well.

Opposite, Rachel Wright, *The Road Less Travelled,* embroidered textile

Jin S. Kim is founding pastor of Church of All Nations and founder of Underground Seminary. This article was written with the help of Isaac Sanborn, who directs youth ministry at Church of All Nations. undergroundsem.org

The Early Church

Rachel
Wright,
*Living on a
Cliff Edge,*
embroidered
textile

What can we learn about reformation today from the early church? The Gospel of Mark opens with John the Baptist proclaiming "repentance and the forgiveness of sins." John was consciously harking back to the traditions of Moses and Elijah, legendary leaders of Israel who practiced the dual roles of prophet and pastor. They boldly entered the courts of Pharaoh and King Ahab and demanded justice. They re-taught the people how to live as family, how to practice hospitality, and how to rely on God for their daily bread. John the Baptist had a simple message: The kingdom of God is just around the corner, so you better get your act together. At the core of his teaching was an ancient biblical ethic of mutual aid and restorative justice: Whoever has two coats must share with anyone who has none; whoever has food must do the same.

Jesus opted to be baptized into the radical wilderness movement that John had faithfully stewarded for years. The Gospels give us a portrait of a scandalously loving and spirit-filled messiah who healed those plagued with evil spirits. He dared feed the hungry whose common lands had been gobbled up by massive estates. He taught the Galileans how to live with one another like Moses had originally taught them. God's law was to love one's neighbors as family, to not scheme about tomorrow, to not give in to the strife and petty jealousies that fracture communities and make them easy to divide and conquer.

When Jesus died, his followers experienced his presence among them. The brutal execution of their Lord could have ended the movement. Instead, they saw that Jesus refused to counter violence with violence. When the women reported an empty tomb, they took it as a sign of Christ's vindication. The story of the resurrection and ascension of the Lord to "the right hand of the Father" became a rallying cry for those who knew Jesus in his life. Jesus had stayed faithful to the Father, the God of his ancestors Abraham, Isaac, and Jacob, even on pain of death. Rome had done its worst, its most terroristic act, and Jesus turned the whole spectacle on its head with the words, "Father, forgive them, for they know not what they do." For the disciples, death had truly lost its sting.

Paul, the "strict constructionist" rabbi who sought to protect the integrity of Pharisaic Judaism by any means necessary, was also a privileged Roman citizen. He was interrupted on his way to Damascus by the stark presence of the resurrected Messiah. Blinded by the Lord's presence, Paul went from being the chief enforcer of temple law to "least of the apostles." As an alternative to Caesar's patronage in the imperial *familia,* Paul could now offer a place in the loving family of God, the body of Christ.

The church has been a force for good in countless ways, and it is right for Christians to celebrate that heritage. But an honest accounting also requires us to admit that for most of its history the institutional church has in alternating ways been both the master and servant of Western empires. Is there another way? Can modern disciples truly follow the Way of Jesus over the American Way?

A New Generation

The church continues only as the next generation accepts the call to be Christ's body, and his hands and feet to the world. As a pastor in a mainline church for twenty-five years, I have noted the dwindling numbers of young people in the local church. The children of boomers see the church today as complicit in, and co-opted by, the ways of the world. They have little interest in perpetuating the Constantinian arrangement in which churches produce loyal foot soldiers for the empire du jour.

The Protestant Reformation and the Radical Reformation were supposed to inaugurate a new era of integrity and faithfulness for the church. But today we see that, whether a congregation is Lutheran, Methodist, Baptist, Quaker, Mennonite, or Presbyterian, they are overwhelmingly white, old, and declining. Such is the fruit of the Reformation after five hundred years.

The church I currently serve was founded in 2004 with a demographic of mostly Korean-American immigrants raised in this country, roughly twenty-five to thirty-five years old. In recent years, CAN has become a slightly majority-white church, although our members

> **For most of its history the institutional church has been both the master and servant of Western empires.**

Rachel Wright, *The Street*, embroidered textile (detail)

still hail from over twenty-five nations and cultures. The one thing that hasn't changed is that two-thirds of our congregation is made up of twenty- to forty-year-olds. Ministering to a mostly millennial congregation has given us some insights about the future of the church in a postmodern context.

What is it that our young people don't buy anymore?

1. Uncritical patriotism and American exceptionalism ("my country, right or wrong").

2. Unexamined white supremacy, both the nativism of the Right and the paternalism toward people of color by the Left.

3. Unfettered consumerism at the expense of global fairness and environmental sustainability, and endless consumption as a personal coping mechanism.

4. Rugged individualism and the subtext of the American dream – the accumulation of enough skills and wealth so as to be completely independent.

5. Christian denominational sectarianism, parochialism, and triumphalism in the face of religious pluralism.

Young people today are desperate for what only the church can offer:

1. Our young people are searching for their vocation. Many are educated enough for a job or career in the present order, but are desperately searching for a calling.

2. Our young people hunger for healthy relationships, to meaningfully and deeply relate to another human being (half grew up in divorced or single-parent homes, and others in dysfunctional households).

3. Plagued with loneliness, isolation, and alienation, our young people are seeking enduring Christian community that functions like a diverse yet intimate family.

4. Our young people are looking for stability in a highly mobile world, and concreteness in an increasingly virtual and socially networked existence.

5. Our young people desire authentic faith. They are prone to agnosticism or even raw atheism, as they see little evidence of a God that makes a difference in the religious institutions of the day, namely the local church. If local churches would respond evangelically to these needs, they would open the possibility of spiritual renewal for this searching but confused generation.

A New Reformation

Many professional religious leaders are working tirelessly for the church's "renewal," hoping that a new reformation might save the institutional church from demise. But people today are not interested in institutional scorekeeping like membership, attendance, budgets, and square feet. If the only motivation for reformation is preserving a middle-class lifestyle for the clergy and preventing the

sanctuary from turning into a condo, then people are saying, Let the temple be torn down, for Jesus can raise it up in three days. Amen, so be it.

We firmly believe that, after five hundred years, the Protestant Reformation is giving way to another tectonic shift in what it means to be church. A new reformation is coming indeed.

One element of that reformation will be learning to live together in intentional Christian community. Our congregation has been forming households of unrelated people almost from our beginning, and now we have multiple community houses that are structured, ordered, and thriving. We were making steady progress, or so we thought, until we began to learn about the Bruderhof way.

We were blown away by this community that goes back almost a hundred years – the lifelong commitment to the community, the common purse, working for businesses that are owned and operated by the overall community, the care of its members from cradle to grave (if they choose to stay). CAN is in the Twin Cities of Minnesota, a highly urbanized area, and cannot as yet match these characteristics. But we have been inspired by an actual community that has done it and is living out the Acts 2 way of being church – of sharing all things in common in an age of individualism, greed, loneliness, and despair.

For us, a radical reformation in our time demands that the church live into its vocation as *ecclesia*, meaning the "called-out ones." Christians are to be called out of a sick society

built on the evils of racism, sexism, militarism, exploitation, and destructive competition. We are to create a new community of love. This does not mean withdrawal from society or indulging sectarian impulses. Church of All Nations is in the middle of an urban and suburban landscape, and hopes to witness to God's love for the world, right here where we are.

With this goal, we seek to pool our people's resources, talents, ideas, and labor for the common good. We want our members to feel that their work is rewarding, that the fruit of their labor is being shared justly, that they work together, live together, play together, and worship together because it is very good and pleasant when kindred live together in unity. We will have to participate in the broader economic system, but we will not allow capitalist dogma to influence our internal economics. We will draw people from our immediate context of great brokenness, but our mission will include the casting out of imperial demons and the healing of bodies and souls so that we can relate rightly to our God, our neighbors (human and non-human), and God's good green earth. We aspire to create an urban village founded on the love and teachings of Jesus Christ our Lord, a type of Bruderhof in the city, and to share God's abundance with an impoverished world.

Is this part of the next reformation, or just a pipe dream? We're not sure, but we are grateful for the witness of the Bruderhof, and pray that Christians can live together in harmony as a counter-witness to a world falling apart. ⟶

The Unplanned Church

How a Brazilian congregation finds renewal by interruption

CLAUDIO OLIVER

When *people say* that we need to be like the "primitive church," I usually ask, "which one?": carnal like the Corinthians, foolish like the Galatians, lazy like the Thessalonians, legalistic like Jerusalem, or lukewarm like the Laodiceans?

Nostalgia is a dangerous path when we start thinking about the reformation we need now. Idealizing the church's "good old times" makes us forget that time erases bad memories and creates fantasies.

The early church survived by keeping its eyes on the promise and living by hope – and we can do the same today. We have been promised to live *with* the Lord, see him face to face, and live in freedom and joy.

During apostolic times, Peter, John, and Paul – and Martin Luther, Jakob Hutter, and Menno Simons during the Reformation – all chose to live in tension, keeping their eyes on Jesus in expectation and aligning themselves with the life that had been promised. Each

---

Claudio Oliver is a founding member of Casa da Videira, an urban farming community in Curitiba, Brazil, whose mission is to live sustainably, serve their neighborhood, and inspire other churches to find new ways to live out their faith.

decision and act was made considering not the principles and values of the empires of the day or of the good old days, but the fullness of the kingdom to come. They tried not to emulate the past but to anticipate the future. Eventually, this brought persecution, misunderstanding, and pain.

We do not plan for reform. On the contrary, the kingdom interrupts our plans, and, if we are open to its message, points us to true renewal. In our community in Brazil, we have been interrupted over and over, and have tried to take steps that will keep us open to God's interruptions.

Our first step was to examine ourselves instead of criticizing others. If the church needed to be reformed, it should begin with us. And we started that by asking some key questions.

The first question was, "If we went off the grid and there were no gas, would what we call 'church' continue?" The plain answer was no. With no energy for sound equipment, projectors, and lights, attendance would go down. With no gas to cross the city to get together once a week, we would have no meeting at all. Something was wrong. We looked back two generations, to when it was possible to gather just by walking, and a word jumped to mind: community. We unplugged our services, moved our meetings to homes, and eventually closed the church building to gather instead where we could be seen by neighbors and friends in our daily life.

Next, we decided to deeply examine each of our programs. If Jesus was not at the very center of any of these, we would close it. We ended up closing 90 percent of what we called "programs." We focused on building relationships based on something that was at the very center of our genesis as a local church: meeting Jesus in the lives of those we were serving. We had been on the streets years earlier to meet Jesus in the homeless people of our city. Rather than helping the poor, our goal was to have a close encounter with those Jesus loves the most. In those men and women, we met a fragile, sometimes difficult, and challenging Jesus. It is impossible to meet Jesus and continue to be the same. Some of them changed, but we changed the most.

Our third question was, "Are we obeying the Lord, and, if not, where should we start?" With a childlike mind, we went back to the Bible, to the first task given to humankind. The Hebrew words *avad* and *shamar* (Gen. 2:15), to serve and to conserve, jumped out at us. That was one of God's first commands. How could we be so concerned about the small specks in our brothers' and sisters' eyes if we were not able to take care of the basic orders given, which were there as planks in front of our eyes? Awareness of creation theology and its consequences became central to our minds. Observing the way that the Lord has created the earth, plants, animals, and us – integrated, not dissociated, as is the schizophrenic pattern of the modern Western mind – to honor and please him led us to creation care as part of the restoration promised in Isaiah. Although we live in a broken world, we choose to live in a regenerative way, taking care of soil, plants, animals, and one another. By refusing to call the creation "natural resources," we also learn how to approach our fellow human beings: not as "human resources" but as the image and resemblance of God, with dignity and a longing for restoration.

By obeying a simple order to tend a garden we learned that we must take seriously the care of our fellow human beings, and as we

We do not plan for reform. The kingdom interrupts our plans.

experimented with setting ourselves limits, we were led to greater freedom. Learning to renounce the seductive offerings of the world by saying, "Thanks but no thanks," even inside our limits, gave us more time and opportunities to build families, friendship, and freedom.

Finally, we asked: "Does this make sense?" Jesus is the answer to all questions, but we must listen, taste, smell, and see the questions being asked in the milieu around us. My grandparents were pioneers of the Salvation Army in Brazil. From them, I learned the meaning of

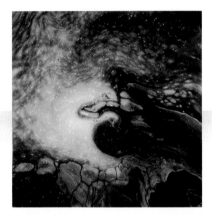

Arthur Brouthers, *Natural Forces*

"good news": my grandfather used to say that good news for a hungry man is a plate of hot soup; for a dirty lady, a place to bathe and rest; for an unemployed boy, a chance to work; for an immigrant, a warm welcome. He had become a refugee at age five during World War I when the family was expelled from Spain for "anarchism and the forbidden practice of Protestantism." Later they lost everything in Belgium during a German bombing, including my great grandfather, who died trying to escape. When they were received by the Salvation Army in

The Church That Grew without Trying

ALAN KREIDER

We tend to forget how surprising the growth of the early church was. Nobody had to join the churches. People were not compelled to become members by invading armies or the imposition of laws; social convention did not induce them to do so. Indeed, Christianity grew despite the opposition of laws and social convention. These were formidable disincentives. In addition, the possibility of death in persecution loomed over the pre-Constantinian church, although few Christians were actually executed.[1] In many places baptismal

candidates sensed that "every Christian was by definition a candidate for death."[2]

Nevertheless the churches grew.[3] Why? After AD 312, when the emperor Constantine I aligned himself with Christianity and began to promote it, the church's growth is not hard to explain. But before Constantine the expansion is improbable enough to require a sustained attempt to understand it. The growth was odd. According to the evidence at our disposal, the expansion of the churches was not organized, the product of a mission program;

Alan Kreider (1941–2017) was professor of church history and mission at Anabaptist Mennonite Biblical Seminary. This article is adapted from his book The Patient Ferment of the Early Church: The Improbable Rise of Christianity in the Roman Empire *(Baker, 2016). See review on page 66.*

Switzerland, my grandfather found family, love, shelter, food, a call, and a ministry; eventually he founded his own missionary family in Brazil. From him, I learned to listen to the questions around me, and yes, Jesus is the answer, but he shows up in different ways: healing, sheltering, planting, feeding, and counseling. He is always present through his body, the church, always manifested in different gifts and talents, asking first, answering later.

We started our community as a typical

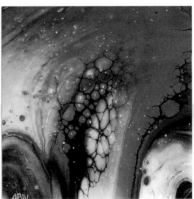

Arthur Brouthers, *Organic Elements*

"seeker-sensitive church" in the early nineties. That approach attracted people, and our attendance grew in a whirlwind of enthusiasm. But soon we perceived that that was exactly the problem: it was all about us. We had become a postmodern religious organization.

The path of questioning and reforming ourselves wasn't a great march to victory, but a great reduction. The more questions we asked, the less we were considered a place to go for religious services. Eventually, we moved back to the streets, to neighbors and people around us. The

....

The expansion of the churches was not organized – it simply happened.

....

it simply happened. Further, the growth was not carefully thought through. Early Christian leaders did not engage in debates between rival "mission strategies." The Christians wrote a lot; according to classicist Robin Lane Fox, "most of the best Greek and Latin literature which remains [from the later second and third centuries] is Christian."[4] And what they wrote is surprising. The Christians wrote treatises on patience – three of them. But they did not write a single treatise on evangelism. Further, to assist their growing congregations with practical concerns, the Christians wrote "church orders," manuals that provided guidance for the life and worship of congregations. The best treatment of how a second-century Christian

should persuade a pagan to become a believer was published in London in 1970![5]

Most improbable of all, the churches did not use their worship services to attract new people. In the aftermath of the persecution of Nero in AD 68, churches around the empire – at varying speeds in varying places – closed their doors to outsiders. By the end of the second century, most of them had instituted what liturgical scholars have called the *disciplina arcani,* the "discipline of the secret," which barred outsiders from entering "private" Christian worship services and ordered believers not to talk to outsiders about what went on behind the closed doors.[6]

(continued)

power of a tiny mustard seed became real to us. As our attendance shrank, our influence grew. People, mostly non-churchgoers, in the city, in the state, all over Brazil, and even overseas started paying attention to what was happening to our insignificant little flock. Broken people from many different backgrounds started coming. We were no longer a place to go, but a people to meet. We rediscovered the church as "a place where the foolish can gather," as Ivan Illich describes it; and we rediscovered that "God chose what is foolish in the world to shame the wise; God chose what is weak in the world to shame the strong; God chose what is low and despised in the world, things that are not, to reduce to nothing things that are, so that no one might boast in the presence of God" (1 Cor. 27–29). The outcome was a community of followers offering communion to anyone in need of being restored.

I think that sometimes Christians seem to know too much after too little observation and careful consideration of the struggles and pain of our times. Our "isms" – nationalism,

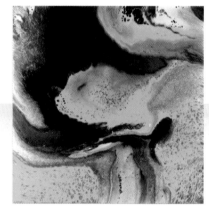

Arthur
Brouthers,
*Unseen
Change*

The early Christians attributed the church's growth to the patient work of God.

(continued from previous page)
Fear motivated this closing – fear of people who might disrupt their gatherings or spy on them. By the third century, some churches assigned deacons to stand at the doors, monitoring the people as they arrived. It is not surprising that pagans responded to their exclusion from Christian worship by speculation and gossip.[7] The baptized Christians, on the other hand, knew how powerful the worship services were in their own lives – early fourth-century North African believers said simply, "We cannot go without the Lord's Supper." They knew that worship services were to glorify God and edify the faithful, not to evangelize outsiders.[8]

And yet, improbably, the movement was growing. In number, size, and geographical spread, churches were expanding without any of the probable prerequisites for church growth. The early Christians noted this with wonder and attributed it to the patient work of God.[9] Teaching catechumens in Caesarea around AD 240, Origen observed that throughout history God had been faithful to Israel, sending them prophets, turning them back from their sins.

> See how great the harvest is, even though there are few workers. But also in another way God plans always that the net is thrown on the lake of this life, and all kinds of fish are caught. He sends out many fishers, he sends out many hunters, they hunt from every hill. See how great a plan it is concerning the salvation of the nations.[10]

The churches grew because the faith that these fishers and hunters embodied was attractive capitalism, conservatism, progressivism, or idealism – set the agenda more than embracing contingencies. And that was another important point in our internal reformation.

As explained by Illich, the parable of the good Samaritan throws light on a forgotten aspect of the Christian life: *corruptio optimi pessima est,* the corruption of the best is the worst. Love is the best expression and the very essence of God. When we corrupt love into obligation instead of the natural flowing that comes out of mercy, we transform the very essence of the gospel into something institutional and cold. In Luke 10:30–37, Jesus teaches us a deep lesson, a key to understanding the very principle of Jesus' ministry – responding to the unexpected.

Strategic planning, never taught as a principle in the Bible, is at the very center of much of the work of today's churches. Goals, missions, plans, and budgets are set, and all contingencies are avoided. Essentially, there's nothing wrong with this, but what did we learn from that parable? The Samaritan was not obliged to do

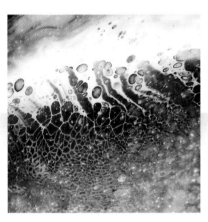

Arthur Brouthers, *Aerial View of Impermanence, III* (detail)

"We do not speak great things but we live them." —Cyprian

to people who were dissatisfied with their old cultural and religious habits, who felt pushed to explore new possibilities, and who then encountered Christians who embodied a new manner of life that pulled them toward what the Christians called "rebirth" into a new life.[11]

Twenty-first-century Christians must live with this heritage. We will not do things precisely as the early Christians did, but the early believers may give us new perspectives and point us to a "lost bequest."[12] As we rediscover this bequest, we will not make facile generalizations or construct how-to formulas. Instead, we will say with Cyprian and other early Christians: "We do not speak great things but we live them."[13] ➤

1. *Apostolic Tradition* 19.2; Cyprian, *To Quirinius* 3.16–18; *Didascalia apostolorum* 5.6.2. Footnotes are abridged in this excerpt; for the full notes, see Alan Kreider, *The Patient Ferment of the Early Church* (Baker, 2016).

2. Gustave Bardy, *La conversion au christianisme durant les premiers siècles* (Aubier, 1949), 170.

3. For an overview, see *The Oxford Handbook of Early Christian Studies,* ed. Susan Ashbrook Harvey and David Hunter (Oxford, 2008), 283–386.

4. Robin Lane Fox, *Pagans and Christians* (Harper & Row, 1986), 270.

5. Michael Green, *Evangelism in the Early Church* (Hodder & Stoughton, 1970), chaps. 3, 5–6.

6. Edward Yarnold, *The Awe-Inspiring Rites of Initiation* (St. Paul, 1971), 50–51.

7. Minucius Felix, *Octavius* 9.3.

8. *Acts of the Abitinian Martyrs* 12.

9. Norbert Brox, "Zur christlichen Mission in der Spätantike," in *Mission im Neuen Testament* (Herder, 1982), 207.

10. Origen, *Homilies on Jeremiah* 18.5.3, trans. J. C. Smith.

11. Justin, *First Apology* 61.3–4, 10; Cyprian, *To Donatus* 3–4.

12. Roger Dowley, *Towards the Recovery of a Lost Bequest* (Evangelical Coalition for Urban Mission, 1984).

13. Cyprian, *On the Good of Patience* 3.

good. He permitted himself to be touched by the suffering of a fellow human and responded using what he had at hand. He didn't ask questions – he loved and acted.

Jesus illustrated the same principle in Luke 8:40–56. He was in the middle of a celebration when he received a call to see a very sick girl.

Paul Cézanne, *Still Life with Seven Apples*

INSIGHTS FROM THE EARLY CHURCH

Christianity is not a matter of persuasive words. It is a matter of true greatness as long as it is hated by the world.

—Ignatius, *Letter to the Romans* 3:2

The Church . . . was created before all things; therefore she is old, and for her sake the world was formed.

—Hermas, *The Shepherd* 8:1

Therefore prepare for action and serve God in fear and truth, leaving behind the empty and meaningless talk and the error of the crowd, and believing in the one who raised our Lord Jesus Christ from the dead and gave him glory and throne at his right hand.

—Polycarp, *Letter to the Philippians* 2:1

He immediately left the crowd to go to her, but even as he was responding to this emergency, he allowed himself to be interrupted again, this time by a woman who had been bleeding for twelve years. He stopped to heal the woman, and set back on his way to the girl. On his way, someone said it was not necessary anymore . . . the girl had died. Even under those circumstances he went and resurrected her, bringing praise and joy to that house.

Even after this demonstration, a religious man asked him: "Who is my neighbor?" The parable was his answer. How many times does our focus on strategic objectives blind us to our neighbor?

Reform in its original (Lutheran) Protestant sense was about what it meant to be catholic (universal). One generation later it was about what it meant not to be Catholic. For many today, "reform" tends to mean, "If you don't agree with our way of doing church, we will just break away and do our thing." Which, ironically, leaves being "protestant" being mostly "arrogant," as one of my dear friends says. Instead of defining ourselves against some other group, the gospel always invites us to turn the mirror back on ourselves to ask about our own transformation as followers of "the Way."

So, yes, we need a new reformation, but we have learned that the first step is to stop waiting for this to start in others. Instead of criticizing others, we must ask questions of ourselves. We must be ready to offer answers, but only when we have listened to the questions. And most importantly, we must permit God to interfere in our agenda, to interrupt our plans, and to guide us back to his Garden. May he be merciful and gracious and bring the reformation we need, starting where we are. ⤳

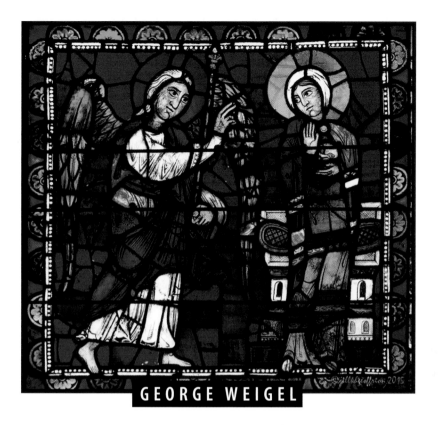

GEORGE WEIGEL

Re-Forming *the* Church

cclesia semper reformanda: the Church always to be reformed. Well, of course. But today, as always, the question is, what makes for authentic reform in the Church? Perhaps a rabbinical story recounted in a popular 1950s Catholic novel, *The Cardinal,* helps focus the question.

The scene set by author Henry Morton Robinson takes place in a New York hotel, where an early attempt at ecumenical reconciliation and interfaith dialogue, a kind

of parliament of religions, is meeting. After numerous vacuous statements are made by this, that, or the other Christian cleric, an elderly rabbi gets up and tells a story.

There was a king, it seems, who owned a precious diamond that he cherished more than anything else in the world. One day, alas, a clumsy servant dropped the diamond, which was deeply scratched as a result. The finest jewelers in the kingdom were summoned to the palace, but despite their best efforts they

The
Annunciation
Window,
Chartres
Cathedral

George Weigel is Distinguished Senior Fellow at the Ethics and Public Policy Center in Washington, DC, where he holds the William E. Simon Chair in Catholic Studies. His twenty-four books include Evangelical Catholicism: Deep Reform in the 21st-Century Church *and a two-volume biography of Pope Saint John Paul II –* Witness to Hope *and* The End and the Beginning.

could not repair the king's diamond. One day, however, an exceptionally skillful jeweler wandered into the kingdom and learned of the sad condition of the king's diamond. He volunteered his services – and by his marvelous, almost miraculous, craftsmanship, he carved onto the diamond a beautiful rose, rendering the deepest part of the scratch the rose's stem.

In the novel, the rabbi does not explicate his parable. But its meaning for a proper understanding of *ecclesia semper reformanda* should be obvious enough. All true reform in the Church is by reference to what is deepest in the Church: the "form" or constitution, which I use in its British, not American, sense, given to the Church by Christ the Lord. That deep "form" is the root from which the disfigurement of the Church can be transformed into renewal and reform.

Authentic Christian reform, in other words, is not a matter of human cleverness, and still less of human willfulness. If the Church is willed by Christ and empowered by the Holy Spirit, then authentic reform means recovering – making a source of renewal – some aspect or other of the Church's "form" that has been lost, marred, misconceived, or even forgotten. Authentic reform means reaching back and bringing into the future something that has been lost in the Church's present. Authentic ecclesial reform is always *re-form*.

A Recent Example

We can see this process of re-forming the Church in late-twentieth-century Catholicism's embrace of religious freedom at the Second Vatican Council, and in the intellectual reclamation project that prepared the way for the Council's *Declaration on Religious Freedom*.

For a variety of historical reasons, including the Reformation and the wars of religion, early-modern Catholic church–state theory favored a confessional state in which political authority was wedded to spiritual authority and the state supported, promoted, and in some instances even enforced the Catholic Church's truth claims. Buttressing this institutional arrangement was a rationale: "error has no rights." The net result was what came to be known as the "thesis/hypothesis" model. The preferred arrangement, in which the Catholic Church enjoyed both the legal protection and financial support of the state, was the "thesis." Over against this thesis stood the "hypothesis": the confessionally neutral state, which could be tolerated if that was what historical contingency demanded.

Various new developments called this thesis/hypothesis model into question. Secularization in Europe in the nineteenth and twentieth centuries had not abated in countries where the Church still enjoyed state favor. There was the counter-experience of the United States, where the confessionally neutral state turned out to be very good for the Church, which was prospering and growing even as established churches in Europe were dying. And so Catholic reformers began to think what had once seemed unthinkable: that maybe establishment is a snare and delusion. If establishment sapped the Church's evangelical energies, perhaps the marriage of spiritual and political authority wasn't such a good idea after all. Concurrently, the notion that "error has no rights" began to be critiqued by theologians who insisted that persons had rights, even if their opinions were erroneous.

Above all, however, the reform of Catholic church–state theory that resulted in Vatican II's *Declaration on Religious Freedom* was due to a reclamation of a gospel truth that had, somehow, been lost in the flux of history: the act of faith, to be authentic, must be a free act. Coerced faith is no faith, or at best faux faith. "God wishes to be adored by people who are free," as the Congregation for the Doctrine of the Faith would later put it in the *Instruction on Christian Freedom and Liberation*.

century and invites all into the fellowship of his friends. A constantly re-forming Church is a Church always seeking the face of the Lord. Friendship with Jesus Christ is not only the beginning of the Church, but also the beginning of all authentic reform in the Church.

Reform means reaching back and bringing into the future something that has been lost in the Church.

That understanding of the nature of faith – a free embrace of the offer of friendship and communion with the Son of God – is part of the Church's Christ-given "form." Retrieving it, and then applying it to contemporary social and political life, made the 1965 *Declaration on Religious Freedom* possible. The Catholic Church did not embrace religious freedom as a basic human right because it finally surrendered to Enlightenment political theory. The Catholic Church's affirmation of religious freedom was an authentic reform that re-formed Catholic church–state theory by retrieving a lost element of the Church's constitutive form and using that element as a means of genuine renewal.

Back to the Future

 s in every other moment in the Church's history, living the motto *ecclesia semper reformanda* in the twenty-first century will mean returning to the sources, the roots, of Christian faith.

This means, first of all, deepening the encounter with Jesus Christ. As Pope Benedict XVI never tired of repeating, Christianity does not begin with an idea or a program but with a person: the Second Person of the Holy Trinity, who walks along the Emmaus Roads of this

And as the Fathers of the Second Vatican Council taught, not least in their efforts to return the Bible to its rightful place in the Catholic Church's life, meeting the Lord means meeting him in his word, the revealed word of God in Holy Scripture. For from that meeting, we learn to see the world aright.

Original sin, we might say, is both the original myopia and the original astigmatism. Because of original sin, we see the world askew: the myopia of original sin gives us a squinty-eyed and narrow view of the world and ourselves, while the astigmatism of original sin further blurs and distorts our vision. In order to see the world (and ourselves) aright, we need corrective lenses. Those lenses are ground by an immersion in the Bible, through which we learn to see the world (and ourselves) in proper focus.

This is especially urgent in times of cultural confusion like our own. The culture of Me – the culture of the imperial autonomous Self, the culture of freedom understood as license and willfulness – envelopes the twenty-first-century West like a dense fog. Seeing through that fog requires a visual acuity that the world can not give. Seeing the world through biblical lenses – through the "inversions" of the Beatitudes, for example – cures our personal myopias and astigmatisms so that the deep truths of the human condition come into clearer focus.

Helping the people of the Church see the world aright through biblical lenses is the first task of the Church's preachers, and thus renewing homiletics must always be part of any authentic ecclesial reform. Preaching-as-therapy, preaching-as-political-education, even preaching-as-moral-exhortation – none of these is adequate to the homiletic task in a reforming Church today. If we would look for models of how expository, biblically rich preaching ought to be done, we can look to another root of the faith once delivered to the saints: the sermons of the great Church Fathers. They, too, sought to help their people see the world of late antiquity, in which old certainties and venerable institutions were crumbling, aright. Their world was not all that different from ours, in which truth is subjectivized and institutions once thought to be built into the human condition (like marriage and the family) are being deconstructed. And so immersion in patristic preaching can be a way to retrieve another lost element of the Church's form and make it into a source of renewal.

Smaller and Purer?

 hen Joseph Ratzinger was elected Bishop of Rome on April 19, 2005, both those who applauded the conclave's decision and those who deplored it dusted off their copies of a small book of the new pope's essays, *Faith and the Future,* and made a beeline for its last chapter, "What Will the Church Look Like in 2000?" There, both Ratzinger fans and Ratzinger critics found the passages that have become perhaps the most frequently cited of this great theologian's voluminous works:

From the crisis of today the Church of tomorrow will emerge – a Church that has lost much. She will become small and will have to start afresh more or less from the beginning. She will no longer be able to inhabit many of the edifices she built in prosperity. As the number of her adherents diminishes, so she will lose many of her social privileges. In contrast to an earlier age, she will be seen much more as a voluntary society, entered only by free decision. As a small society, she will make much bigger demands on the initiative of her individual members. . . . But in all the changes at which one might guess, the Church will find her essence afresh and with full conviction in that which was always at her center: faith in the triune God, in Jesus Christ, the Son of God made man, in the presence of the Spirit until the end of the world. . . .

But when the trial of this sifting is past, a great power will flow from a more spiritualized and simplified Church. Men in a totally planned world will find themselves unspeakably lonely. If they have completely lost sight of God, they will feel the full horror of their poverty. Then they will discover the little flock of believers as something wholly new. They will discover it as a hope that is meant for them, an answer for which they have always been searching in secret.

No serious Christian theologian, and certainly no pope, wants to shrink the Church: that we may take as axiomatic. What Ratzinger was outlining here was not a plan, but the reality of *ecclesia semper reformanda* in the late-modern and postmodern West. Genetically transmitted Christianity – the faith passed along by ethnic custom – was finished. Virtually no one in the Church of the twenty-first century, Ratzinger saw in 1970, would be able to answer the question, "Why are you a Christian?" by replying,

"Because my great-grandmother was born in Bavaria" (or County Cork, or Cracow, or Guadalajara, or Palermo – or even South Boston). The only faith possible under late-modern and postmodern conditions is faith freely embraced in a free decision, made possible by the lives of the walking wounded of the post-modern world, and thereby offer what the world has been searching for, if unwittingly: friendship with Jesus Christ, who is the answer to the question that is every human life, and incorporation into the communion of his friends.

What the twenty-first-century Church needs most are witnesses: men and women on fire with missionary zeal.

an encounter with the risen Lord, Jesus Christ. Therefore, whatever institutions of ecclesial life would remain after what Ratzinger dubbed "the trial of this sifting" (which he believed had been underway for more than a century) would have to reconceive themselves as launching pads for mission, communities where those who had received the gift of faith would have to learn how to offer it to others. That gift would not bring with it, as in the past, social status. But it would bring something far more important: it would bring hope, rooted in faith and exercised in charity.

Both Ratzinger's papal predecessor and his papal successor have shared this vision, if with different accents. John Paul II called Catholicism – and by extension, all of Christianity – into a "New Evangelization" whose biblical metaphor was Luke 5:4: the Church must leave the shallow and brackish waters of institutional maintenance and, like the disciples on the Sea of Galilee, "put out into the deep" – the roiling, storm-tossed waters of a world that has lost its bearings. In what he has called the grand strategy document of his papacy, *Evangelii Gaudium* (The Joy of the Gospel), Pope Francis struck a similar note, calling for a "Church permanently in mission" in which the nobility of life displayed by Ratzinger's "little flock of believers" would touch

All of which is to say that the reformation we need at this quincentenary of Wittenberg is a re-formed Church of saints. The cultural dissolution of the West precludes arguing people into the faith. Very few people are going to be argued into belief in a world that accepts "your truth" and "my truth," but not *the* truth. Yes, the Church needs theologians. Yes, the Church needs fully catechized men and women who can make persuasive arguments, but what the reformed Church of the twenty-first century needs most are witnesses: men and women on fire with missionary zeal, because they have been embraced by the love of Christ and are passionate to share that love with others; men and women who see the world through a biblical optic; men and women sanctified by the sacraments; men and women who know, with Saint Paul, that the trials of the present age are preparing within the *ecclesia semper reformanda* an "eternal weight of glory" (2 Cor. 4:17). ➤

The Renegade Monk

Martin Luther's Battle for the Freedom of Faith

Five hundred years ago . . .

The year is 1517; the place, Wittenberg, Germany. It is an age of anxiety. Poverty, hunger, and political unrest are widespread; periodic plagues kill untold thousands; public executions attract enormous crowds. Fearing death, the devil, and the agonies of purgatory, crowds of people seek absolution through pilgrimage and penance. Smelling an opportunity, Jakob Fugger, a powerful Augsburg banker, collaborates with the Vatican in the sale of indulgences, paper certificates purporting to grant the buyer a waiver from post-mortem punishment for sins.

Born in 1483 in Eisleben, Germany, Martin Luther has received a Master of Arts degree at the University of Erfurt, and then dropped out of law school to become a monk. A pilgrimage to Rome has only intensified his brooding doubts and fears. Now, after years of frustrated seeking, the young monk has just broken through to the bold new insight that will define his life mission: faith, not works, absolves sins; salvation is ours through God's grace alone.

Taken from Renegade, Andrea Grosso Ciponte and Dacia Palmerino's new graphic biography, the following pages depict Luther's first forays into the conflict that would define the 16th century.

Andrea Grosso Ciponte, artist, *is a Calabrian painter, graphic novelist, and filmmaker, as well as a professor of digital animation techniques at the Academy of Fine Arts in Catanzaro, Italy.* ***Dacia Palmerino, writer,*** *researches audiovisual and multimedia art and curates film and video exhibits.*

... All descendants of Adam are corrupted by sin. Only faith in God through Jesus Christ can free us. Not pilgrimages, not fasting, not saints or relics: we are saved by faith alone.

My son, I have not seen you at Mass for a long time. Would you like to go to confession?

That is no longer necessary, Father Luther. The Pope has absolved me from my sins!

What's going on here? Have you wasted your few pennies on a worthless piece of paper? Who sold it to you?

Father Johann Tetzel. Many of us have moved to Magdeburg to receive grace from His Holiness ... In doing so, we have contributed to the construction of St. Peter's!

Have you covered the relics of a saint with gold because you believe it will save you from Purgatory?

55

What does the sign say?

I don't know, it's in Latin!

"The Pope can not remit any guilt ...!" What a bold idea. Everyone must take note of this.

"The Pope cannot remit any guilt; except by declaring and showing that it has been remitted by God!"

Thanks to the recent invention of the printing press, the 95 Theses spread quickly and were immediately translated into German, so that everyone could understand them.

"Christians are to be taught that he who gives to the poor or lends to the needy does a better deed than he who buys indulgences."

latein grammatik

"Those who say that the soul flies out of purgatory as soon as the coin falls into the coffer are preaching lies and deceit."

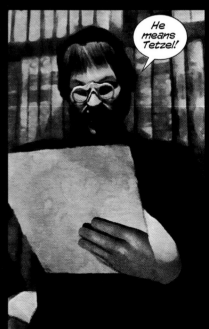

He means Tetzel!

It is a very delicate moment, Your Holiness. The unity of all Catholic countries must be preserved. This monk has enflamed tempers across the entire German Empire, and meanwhile the Turks are approaching.

Obviously all our warnings have achieved nothing. What is Elector Frederick of Saxony thinking in not restraining this hothead?

Perhaps he wants to be the only German prince who is allowed to fleece his subjects?

The Holy Inquisition, Your Holiness ...

Yes, the Holy Inquisition! Luther must be charged, and then we will see who has the last word — a little arrogant German monk or Christ's vicar on earth!

You'll see, as soon as he faces being handed over to the secular authorities for punishment, he will recant everything ...

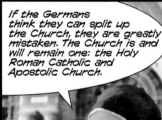

I certainly hope so, for his sake.

If the Germans think they can split up the Church, they are greatly mistaken. The Church is and will remain one: the Holy Roman Catholic and Apostolic Church.

Leipzig University, July 1519. Luther, accompanied by fellow professors Philip Melanchthon and Andreas Karlstadt, has arrived with 200 Wittenberg students for a 14-day disputation on his 95 Theses. His chief opponent is Dr. Johann Eck, a defender of the Pope. The debate brings much publicity for Luther's views.

The Pope and the councils cannot err in matters of faith or doctrine.

We should justify the actions of the Pope through the Scriptures alone ...

The councils too can err!

There he is, the revolutionary! Do you realize the gravity of your words?

Neither the Pope nor the council has the ultimate authority in matters of faith. Even Jan Hus ...

Jan Hus? Are you now invoking a heretic in this matter?

He too was telling the truth! It's not a question of heresy but of Christian teachings! The papacy bases its "authority" solely on its power to excommunicate!

Martin Luther, you are pushing for a split that cannot be reversed. You deny the authority of the Pope and the councils. You have fallen from the faith!

Upon returning to Wittenberg, Luther writes three eloquent pamphlets: "To the Christian Nobility of the German Nation," "On the Babylonian Captivity of the Church" and "On the Freedom of a Christian." He sends the latter tract together with a letter to Pope Leo, calling on him to abdicate the papacy. In June 1520, Leo X issues the papal bull "Exsurge Domine" which threatens Luther with excommunication.

BVLLA Decimi Leonis, contra errores Martini Lutheri, & sequacium.

I know what you're thinking, Father Staupitz, I can see it in your eyes.

63

Renegade
Martin Luther: The Graphic Biography
Andrea Grosso Ciponte • Dacia Palmerino

softcover, 156 pages
Plough, October 2017
plough.com/renegade

Five hundred years ago a brash young monk single-handedly confronted the most powerful institutions of his day. His bold stand sparked the Protestant Reformation and marked one of the great turning points in history. Martin Luther, a spiritual and historical giant, is loved and hated to this day – and for good reason.

In this graphic novel, each chapter of Luther's life comes vividly to life thanks to cutting-edge graphic techniques, meticulous historical research, and compelling writing. While squarely confronting the darker aspects of Luther's legacy, it nevertheless shows how one man's courageous stand of conscience ended up changing the world. ⇝

Editors' Picks

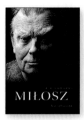

Miłosz: A Biography
Andrzej Franaszek
Edited and translated by
Aleksandra and Michael
Parker (Belknap)

In this newly translated biography, Andrzej Franaszek masterfully compiles and condenses reams of letters, essays, books, and poetry to tell the story of one of the twentieth century's great poets.

Czesław Miłosz, who won the Nobel Prize in Literature in 1980, was born in 1911 in a rural Lithuanian village and spent much of his childhood traveling, as his father was mobilized to build roads for the Russian army. As a young man, he worked in the Polish resistance movement in Nazi-occupied Warsaw during World War II, and later lived in Washington and Paris as a cultural ambassador for Communist Poland. Eventually, unable to live under totalitarian censorship, he defected to the United States and took up teaching at Berkeley.

As he moved from place to place, Miłosz watched the landscape shift, not only geographically but also intellectually and spiritually: fascist and communist regimes in Europe, the vapid consumerism of post-war America, startling technological advances, church reforms, and San Francisco's countercultural movement.

For Miłosz, this constant displacement was a reminder that this life is but an exile from our true home, and his poetry often returns to this theme. Miłosz lived through dark times, and his poetry reflects this, but he never succumbed to despair: "I did not have the makings of an atheist," he wrote, "because I lived in a state of constant wonder, as if before a curtain which I knew had to rise someday." This constant wonder, this hope, and this faith sustained him, and made his poetry luminous and timeless.

> **"I have felt the pull of despair and impending doom. . . . Yet on a deeper level, I believe, my poetry remained sane and, in a dark age, expressed a longing for the kingdom of peace and justice."**
>
> **— Czesław Miłosz**

The Vanishing American Adult: Our Coming-of-Age Crisis – and How to Rebuild a Culture of Self-Reliance
Ben Sasse
(St. Martin's)

It's a national crisis: young people these days just don't want to grow up. But instead of haranguing the kids, Ben Sasse, maverick first-term Republican senator from Nebraska, has some straightforward advice for their parents. Sasse's five proposed character-building habits are simple and actionable: Teach your children to work hard. Have them spend time with their elders. Give them good books. Travel to expand their horizons. And don't live for material gain.

At times Sasse seems to assume his reader shares his privilege – stable family life, secure income, and ample if not limitless opportunity – but there's plenty here of use to anyone. The section on how to find meaningful work for your kids is helpful, especially if you don't have fields to plow or wood to split. (Sasse took flak for sending his fourteen-year-old daughter to work on a ranch.) So is the chapter on over-consumption and teaching the difference between needs and wants. And anyone can encourage the reading of good books. It's not public policy, but rather personal advice, delivered in a conversational, parent-to-parent tone that seems to welcome discussion and even disagreement.

*A Place of Refuge:
An Experiment in Communal
Living – The Story of Windsor
Hill Wood*
Tobias Jones
(Riverrun)

What happens when you open your family home to anyone facing a personal crisis?

Toby and Francesca Jones are not the starry-eyed idealists they were seven years ago, when they decided to start a woodland community on ten acres in Somerset, England – a place of healing for people dealing with addictions, mental illness, eating disorders, and a host of other issues.

Jones offers an honest, sometimes hilarious journal of the first five years of that adventure. A professional journalist, he had previously visited dozens of communities to write *Utopian Dreams,* to which this book is "the hard-bitten response."

An astute observer of nature and human nature, Jones finds the humanity in every misfit who rolls up their gravel drive looking for a home, and beauty in the abandoned quarry they transform into a scrappy farm and productive woodland on a shoestring budget.

They make their mistakes, ride out seasons of disillusionment and exhaustion, learn their limits, and establish guidelines. Through it all, they keep on welcoming a tide of brokenness

that, it seems, no amount of generosity, trust, and affirmation can heal. Or can it? When people step out in faith, miracles often happen.

*The Patient Ferment of the
Early Church: The Improbable
Rise of Christianity in the
Roman Empire*
Alan Kreider
(Baker)

Few new books have been as enthusiastically passed around in the *Plough* office as this overview of Christianity in its first three centuries (see excerpt on pages 40–43). Kreider starts with a historical question: How did the pre-Constantinian church grow, given that new converts faced both social stigma and the real risk of persecution? After all, it's not that the early church made it easy on its recruits, who were expected to adopt a rigorous life of nonviolence, simplicity, and sexual discipline. Nor were early congregations "seeker-friendly": outsiders were banned from attending worship services, and the task of a deacon was less to be a greeter than a bouncer.

So what made people want to join this unpopular group? As Kreider shows, it was the power of example. Christians, though living in the midst of society, formed distinct communities shaped by certain habits: daily prayer, early morning Eucharist, sharing money and food with the needy, making the sign of the cross, giving the fraternal kiss of peace – a scandalous greeting that made visible the equality of all believers, regardless of wealth, race, gender, or status. Kreider's account, vivid with unforgettable details, will prompt many to wonder: Is the shopworn Christianity of our day the real deal, or merely a diluted version of something far harder and nobler? ⤳ *The Editors*

The Last of the First Christians

ANDREAS KNAPP

The ancient Christian communities within Iraq and Syria, decimated by the Islamic State, are on the brink of extinction. Now, with ISIS driven from Mosul, the future of Christianity in the region will likely be decided this autumn, as displaced Christians decide whether to risk returning to their destroyed homes and Muslim neighbors, or leave for good. Andreas Knapp, author of *The Last Christians*, has been working among the uprooted survivors and recording their stories.

An internally displaced child sleeps in St. Joseph's Church, Erbil, Iraq.

T'S BEEN SEVERAL YEARS since I quit my job as director of Freiburg Seminary to live and work among the poor in Leipzig, Germany, along with three other members of the Little Brothers of Jesus, a religious order inspired by Charles de Foucauld. At an open house for our neighbors, many of them refugees from the Middle East, a thickset man of about forty comes up to me. Beside him is a boy with jet-black hair who looks about eleven. Yousif – as the broad-shouldered stranger turns out to be called – addresses me. I don't

understand him, but the boy already speaks excellent German and translates for him, "We are from Iraq, from Mosul. Please help us!"

The tasks awaiting me flash before my eyes: my duties in the parish and as a chaplain at a prison and a college. I feel like saying, "Sorry, I'd love to, but I haven't got time." But I can't do it. The next day, I call to arrange a visit. My life hasn't been the same since.

A few days later, I ring the doorbell of an eleven-story apartment block. Yousif lives on the third floor with his wife, Tara, and their two children, Amanuel and Shaba. They invite me into their living room. Yousif's request for help, I learn, concerns his children. There are problems at school. Amanuel, a slightly built boy, confides to me that he is regularly bullied by his Muslim schoolmates because of the small cross he has always worn around his neck, even when things got dangerous for Christians in Mosul. Spotting it, an older Muslim boy had begun calling him names, then pretended to point a machine gun at him: "Ratatatata! Shoot the Christians!"

Such tensions among refugees are not uncommon. The majority of the more than one million refugees who have entered Germany since 2015 are Muslims. Many of them have also been ideologically poisoned by decades of propaganda claiming that Christians are "impure," that the West is morally corrupt, and that only Muslims can be citizens in the full sense of the word.

Christian refugees are suspected by both sides, as I learn after I arrange for Amanuel to transfer to a Christian school. Here things go better – until he feels suspected by his classmates of being a jihadist. After a terror attack in Paris, the children are afraid that radical Muslims might launch an attack in Germany too. One boy reads out a newspaper headline, "Jihadist Came to France as Refugee," and some of them turn to look at Amanuel.

I ASK YOUSIF – with Amanuel's help – to tell me something of their story. In Mosul, he and Tara had been very involved in the Syrian Orthodox Church. But after 2003, everything changed. In response to the American-led invasion of Iraq, Muslim clerics called for a holy war. Large numbers of fundamentalist jihadists from all over the Islamic world came together to wage war on the "unbelievers." Christians in Iraq became fair game for the Islamists.

In the eyes of many Muslims, Western nations are "Christian" states. In the event of an attack by those states, Christians in the Middle East are suspected of being collaborators and allies of the invaders. The Christians' precarious situation was worsened by a speech by then-president George W. Bush, in which he called his war a "crusade," thereby stirring up deep-seated Muslim resentment against the West. The Iraqi Christians, who had never been involved in a crusade in their two-thousand-year history, were seen as guilty by association and subjected to a regime of terror. They became scapegoats on whom revenge could be exacted for the aggression of the "Christian occupiers." For example, protection money was extorted from Christians by invoking the ancient Islamic practice of levying a special tax, referred to as jizya in the Quran, on non-Muslims. Under Islamic (shari'a) law, Christians must pay jizya for the privilege of being allowed – albeit to a very limited extent – to practice their religion.

According to Yousif, the sums demanded increased year by year. You paid up because you knew what the alternative would be: destruction of your property, and murder. Even Christian churches became targets of the terror perpetrated in the name of Islam. Yet many Christians still wouldn't contemplate leaving Mosul, cherishing the faint hope that the nightmare would come to an end one day. Among these were Yousif and Tara.

Andreas Knapp is a poet, priest, and author living in Leipzig, Germany. His latest book, The Last Christians *(Plough, 2017), recounts the stories of refugees in his neighborhood and of displaced people in camps in Kurdistan, northern Iraq (see opposite).*

Instead, things got even worse. One day, an anonymous caller threatened to cut off Yousif's left arm. He knew immediately what the caller was getting at, as he has a large cross tattooed on his brawny left forearm. "You just try!" Yousif retorted impulsively, and hung up.

It was plain to him that he was living dangerously now, and that his young family was at risk too. A few days later, the phone rang again: "If you're not gone in three days, you will go to hell!" Yousif knew he had to act fast, and left Mosul with his wife and their two children. They made for Erbil, the capital of the autonomous Kurdish region in northern Iraq. There he was safe, but unable to find work. After much agonizing, he made up his mind to flee to Europe, preferably to Germany or Sweden.

T HIS JOURNEY had to be undertaken alone. Though it broke Yousif's heart to leave his wife and children, such a venture was far too hazardous for them, the only route being via the dark machinations of a people-smuggling gang. The price demanded was seventeen thousand US dollars. Yousif sold everything he possibly could and borrowed the rest from friends and relatives. Even now, he tells me, he still owes five thousand.

Yousif was stowed in a hidden compartment of a semitrailer. Seven days later, he heard the truck stop, and the trapdoor was unscrewed and opened. Yousif crawled out, stiff and hardly able to walk. He was in an empty parking lot, lit feebly by a couple of streetlights. It was bitterly cold and there wasn't a sound to be heard apart from the rumble of the engine.

The driver pointed in the direction of the local train station. There Yousif was to wait for a man who would return his passport. Spotting a white license plate in unfamiliar lettering on a passing vehicle, he read: C – Chemnitz. He was in Germany.

Picked up by police and sent to a home for asylum seekers, for the next six months Yousif lived in an agony of uncertainty: Would things remain calm in Erbil? Was there a chance that Tara and the children might be able to come to Germany soon? Would his parents – left behind in Mosul – be put under pressure or even murdered by the jihadists? Such thoughts and fears tortured him night and day. And he felt so helpless in this new country, whose language he didn't understand and whose bureaucracy was a mystery to him. Finally, his asylum application was accepted and he was able to bring Tara, Amanuel, and Shaba over by legal means.

At the same time, his home city of Mosul was occupied by Islamic State militias, forcing his parents, his brother, and all his relatives, along with the entire Christian community, to leave the city and flee to the Kurdish region to

Christian refugees are suspected by both sides.

the north. His father, already in a wheelchair, died in the refugee camp.

A Nonviolent Tradition

As I get to know more Christian refugees from Iraq and Syria, I can't help noticing how often they mention Bible verses about forgiveness, nonviolence, and loving one's enemy. These people have lost family members to terrorists and were robbed of their homes and possessions – and yet, instead of uttering words of revenge or retaliation, they are quoting words of peace from Jesus' Sermon on the Mount.

Shouldn't it be an honor for Christians to show love to our persecutors?

One day I ask Yousif about it: "What's the attitude of Christians in Iraq toward weapons and violence?"

"We reject the use of arms. When my uncle was called up for military service, he was sent directly to the front in the war against Iran, but he always aimed into the distance, asking the Holy Virgin to send the bullet astray."

"Even in the current situation," Yousif adds, "where Christians like us are being driven out of our towns and villages after eighteen or nineteen hundred years, armed resistance is still not an option for us."

I bore deeper into this attitude to life: "You have suffered so much. Why don't you meet violence with violence?"

Without hesitation, Yousif insists, "As Christians, we are not supposed to bear arms. . . . The church has always been clear that war is Satan's work."

"Is there no such thing as Christian jihad?" I ask.

Yousif rejects this emphatically: "Only Muslims have jihad. Our struggle consists of prayer and fasting. Christianity isn't spread by the sword. For terrorists, it's an honor to kill people. Shouldn't it be an honor for us as Christians to show love to our persecutors?"

This attitude, I discover, has deep roots in the Middle Eastern churches. In October 2015, for example, the Russian air force began a series of missions against the Islamic State in Syria. A representative of the Russian Orthodox Church welcomed the deployment as a "holy war." Jacques Behnan Hindo, the Syrian archbishop of Hassaké-Nisibi, criticized this statement in the strongest terms: "As Christians, we cannot talk of a holy war – otherwise what difference would there be between radical Muslims and Christians? Instead, we must make it clear that war is always a sin."

Another bishop, Aprem Athnil, wrote a letter to ISIS leaders stating, "We categorically reject a culture of weapons," and seeking to impress on ISIS that the Christian church is not in alliance with the Kurdistan Workers' Party, or PKK. True, a so-called Christian militia is fighting alongside the PKK to defend or recapture the villages. But although the international press refers to this militia as "Christian," Bishop Aprem protests that it was neither funded nor approved by the church and insists that there can be no armed force in the name of Christianity.

"Muslim militias versus Christian militias" – such simplifications make the world much easier to explain, even if they are far from the whole truth. Clearly, a report on "Christian militias" grabs attention; a sustained tradition of nonviolence in Eastern Christianity is less interesting to write about. Has anyone even noticed that, despite the numerous brutal murders of Christian priests in Iraq and Syria, no imam has ever been shot, beheaded, or crucified in the name of Christianity? Or that no Christians have ever blown themselves up in a mosque in retaliation for the many attacks on Christian churches?

The Islamic State bombs itself into the media, while the far more impressive testimony of nonviolence fails to make the copy desk.

By contrast, it was only after a long process of self-purification that the Roman Catholic Church, for example, has recovered the early Christian teaching on the separation of church and state. This sometimes-bitter learning experience is something that the churches could bring to bear in modern-day interfaith dialogues with Muslims. After all, many Muslims are well aware that, in its current state, Islam suffers from an unhappy entanglement of religion with state power – one of the causes of a long history of excessive violence stretching into the present. In this regard, Middle Eastern churches, which for centuries have not wielded political power, have remained truer to Christianity's nonviolent roots than European Christianity.

Scattered Seeds

Now these Eastern churches are being scattered around the globe. Some of them are perhaps doomed to die out, and if so, Jesus' words may prove true: "Unless a kernel of wheat falls to the ground and dies, it remains only a single seed. But if it dies, it produces many seeds" (John 12:24).

All the more, displaced Christians deserve our full solidarity. Since they have now been dispersed worldwide, we should make it our mission to seek them out and invite them into our communities. We can approach aid agencies in order to locate Middle Eastern Christians and offer them practical assistance with finding accommodation and work. In the case of individuals or families, inviting them to join our local churches would be an important gesture of fellowship. As some of the last people who still speak the language Jesus spoke, they can enrich our church services – by

leading the Lord's Prayer in Aramaic, for instance. If a sizeable group of Eastern Christians can be assembled in a town, we can help them set up a community by offering them our church facilities. That way we can support their efforts to practice the faith that caused them to be expelled in the first place, and to keep their language and traditions alive.

Naturally, it will take time for some Christians from Iraq and Syria to be reconciled with Muslims after having been shamefully betrayed by their Muslim neighbors. All the more, I think with admiration of Rami, a Christian from Mosul whose younger brother was murdered by the jihadists and whose family was driven from their home: now he is giving his time to accompany a Muslim family on visits to the authorities as a volunteer interpreter.

And there are Muslims doing the same. On another visit to Yousif and Tara's house, a Muslim family stops by: a young woman in a headscarf, a tall man, and three small children. They sit on the sofas and Yousif introduces Hamoudi to me: "We were neighbors in Mosul – and very good friends."

Hamoudi tells me how ISIS terrorists captured Yazidi women and children and deported them to Mosul for their "own use," imprisoning them in different houses. Hamoudi managed to rescue a fourteen-year-old girl and

The author and two Little Sisters of Jesus visiting a family from Qaraqosh, Iraq, now living in Iraqi Kurdistan fled with her and his own family to Kurdistan. In my opinion, this man deserves some kind of honor, just as people who rescued Jews in the Third Reich were honored as the "Righteous among the Nations." Because of his brave action, he is now living in exile and cannot return to Mosul.

This story brings home to me yet again how many Muslims have been at the receiving end of Islamist terrorism. Muslims like Hamoudi who crave democracy and respect human rights have been forced to flee their homelands and seek asylum. I know a young Muslim mechanic who fled to Germany in peril of his life rather than work on a project designing car bombs.

> **For Christian refugees, belief in God is not just an intellectual exercise but defines their whole life.**

It saddens and angers me to think of such Muslims becoming victims of blind Islamophobia. At the same time, I am aware that I am not always discerning enough myself. So many Muslims come to Europe precisely because they don't want a Salafist Islam and have suffered greatly from politicized religion. If we can succeed in integrating these people, we will have taken an important step toward increasing the chances that the currents within Islam that reject discrimination and violence in the name of religion will prevail.

YOUSIF AND TARA have found they have much to offer their German neighbors as well as receiving support from them. For nearly a year now, Peter has been coming to help Amanuel and Shaba with their homework. The sixteen-year-old high school student was placed with them via the Leipzig Refugee Council. Yousif tells me that Peter comes much more often than originally arranged. He evidently feels at ease with the family, sometimes popping over for supper and staying late. These visits are a completely new experience for Peter, whose parents separated when he was young. Having often felt pushed from pillar to post and not really at home anywhere, he encounters here the warm hospitality of a Middle Eastern family whose door is always open and for whom it's never any trouble to set an extra place at the table.

Like most Leipzigers, Peter has grown up in an atheist environment and doesn't believe in God. In Tara and Yousif, he has come to know a deeply religious family: the walls are decorated with Christian symbols and grace is said before meals. Above all, however, he has discovered that belief in God is not just an intellectual exercise for Yousif and his family, but something that defines their whole life. They have paid a high price for their Christian faith, losing their home and all their possessions for the sake of Jesus Christ.

This all-engulfing devotion is not something the young Leipziger can relate to, but he understands something of its psychological importance. For these refugees, their faith is a support, buoying them up after all the losses they have suffered. Rather than becoming embittered, they trust that their lives are safe in the hands of a higher power.

Peter has regular discussions with Yousif or Amanuel about the existence of God. For Yousif, too, this is a new experience, since he had never before met anyone who doesn't believe in God. Their conversations are a mutually enriching exchange between believer and nonbeliever. From Christianity's Middle Eastern birthplace, the refugees are bringing faith back to a Europe that has forgotten its roots. ⤳

▶ *Watch a video about Andreas Knapp's new book at* plough.com/lastchristians.

CÉCILE MASSIE

The Church Is Not Made of Cathedrals

Ministering to a Church in Exile

Holy Week 2017, Turkey

In the summer of 2015, Father Jacques Mourad was kidnapped by ISIS from the Monastery of Saint Elian in Al-Qaryatayn, Syria, and held in captivity until his escape five months later (see "An Impossible Hope," Summer 2017). He is one of ten monks and nuns of the community of Mar Musa, which he founded in 1991 with Father Paolo Dall'Oglio, an Italian Jesuit who was kidnapped by ISIS in Raqqa in July

Father Jacques Mourad blesses a young boy in Cappadocia, Turkey.

Cécile Massie, who lives in France, began taking photographs while in Syria in 2010–2011. Since then, she has covered displaced populations in several countries, including Nigeria and Iraqi Kurdistan. She is now devoted to issues related to refugees and interreligious dialogue.

We rolled up the carpets, gathered all the chairs in the house, and laid out the mattresses for the children.

In each city, Father Jacques goes from house to house, Bible in hand, to visit the sick.

2013. The ecumenical community, which practices the Syriac Catholic liturgy, is based in Deir Mar Musa, a monastery that dates from the sixth century. Before the war, the community hosted visitors from all over the world, focusing on interreligious work, specifically Muslim-Christian dialogue.

Now exiled from Syria, Father Jacques has continued his ministry in Iraqi Kurdistan. In April, he traveled with Monsignor Paolo Bizzeti, the Vicar Apostolic of Anatolia, to Cappadocia, Turkey, to serve some 1,200 Iraqi Christian refugees located in five different cities.[1]

Father Jacques and the Christians he visits may not be from the same country but they speak the same language and practice the same rites: Syriac and Chaldean. The families he meets have been in Turkey since the summer of 2014, when they fled the advance of Daesh[2] forces in Iraq. All have requested emigration and are waiting for news. It is almost impossible to establish themselves in Turkey, said one man in Kırşehir: "We face too much discrimination on a daily basis. Finding work is very complicated as an Iraqi Christian. Those who do find work are underpaid."

1. *Editor's note:* Although Cappadocia has been a place of Christian flourishing for millennia – it is mentioned in the First Letter of Peter, and was home to the great fourth-century Church Fathers – there are few functioning churches today.
2. Acronym of the Arabic name for ISIS.

The week unfolds based on needs and opportunities – Masses are organized daily. Because the few local churches have been closed or transformed into coffeehouses or museums, the Masses are said in banquet halls illuminated by disco balls or in family homes. At Nevşehir there are thirty-four worshipers, originating from Bartella, Baghdad, and Mosul. In order to attend the Mass, their first since Christmas, they cram into this narrow room with curtains pulled. Their eagerness to welcome and converse with the two priests reveals the solitude experienced in exile. Father Jacques is a former detainee and a refugee among refugees. His testimony creates a closeness, his strength and peace preaches comfort.

At each location, the two priests visit the sick. Lahib comes from Mosul; he was operated on nine months ago for a brain tumor. When the two priests celebrate Mass at his home, he cries and thanks God that he is able to walk again. On Holy Thursday, Monsignor Bizzeti addresses a gathering of two hundred and fifty Christians in an ornate wedding hall: "The true Church is not made up of cathedrals," he tells them, "but of a community gathered in spite of everything."

Once Mass is over, we leave quickly, as the hall could be rented for only two hours. Outside it is raining, and everyone disperses. A man welcomes the two priests to his home for the evening to discuss the

Father Jacques Mourad and Monsignor Paolo Bizzeti celebrate Mass for Iraqi Christian refugees. The majority of the thirty-four Christians of Nevşehir came to worship in this tiny drawing room.

In the Middle East, children celebrate Easter with hand-painted hard-boiled eggs.

difficulties of the local community. With delicacy and firmness, Bishop Bizzeti tries to restrain their hopes of obtaining visas. "I have great admiration for these men and women who retain a profound faith in such difficult times," he tells me later. "But they must know that only a minority can leave; they have to find the means to live here, today, in this country."

The only room actually serving as a church in the region is on the third floor of a building in the center of Kayseri. The Protestant community has obtained authorization from the authorities to set up a space there. It is here that the Easter Mass is celebrated on a Saturday afternoon. Several make the hour-and-a-half-long bus trip from cities the priests have already visited. This Holy Week is celebrated without cross or procession: like these lives, celebrations have been deprived of ornament. But at the end of every Mass, and especially on this Saturday, joy and gratitude can be read on all faces.

Before he leaves the country, Father Jacques tells me, "These people are here because they are aware of their right to life and have a solid faith. The celebration of the resurrection strengthens the hope that they have in their hearts." ➤

View the rest of this photo series at cecilemassie.com/leglise-nest-faite-de-cathedrales.

(Continued from page 80)

said to him, "Swear and I will release you! Curse Christ!"

Polycarp answered, "Eighty-six years have I served him, and he has never done me any harm. How could I blaspheme my King and Savior?"

When the proconsul still pressed him, saying, "Swear by the genius of Caesar," he replied, "If you desire the empty triumph of making me swear by the genius of Caesar according to your intention, and if you pretend that you do not know who I am, hear my frank confession: I am a Christian. If you are willing to learn what Christianity is, set a time at which you can hear me."

The proconsul replied, "Try to persuade the people." Polycarp answered him, "You I consider worthy that I should give an explanation, for we have been taught to pay respect to governments and authorities appointed by God as long as it does us no harm. But as to that crowd, I do not consider them worthy of my defense."

Thereupon the proconsul declared, "I have wild beasts. I shall have you thrown before them if you do not change your mind."

"Let them come," he replied. "It is out of the question for us to change from the better to the worse, but the opposite is worthy of honor: to turn round from evil to justice."

The proconsul continued, "If you belittle the beasts and do not change your mind, I shall have you thrown into the fire." Polycarp answered him, "You threaten me with a fire that burns but for an hour and goes out after a short time, for you do not know the fire of the coming judgment and of eternal punishment for the godless. Why do you wait? Bring on whatever you will."

As Polycarp spoke these and similar words, he was full of courage and joy. His face shone with inward light. He was not in the least disconcerted by all these threats. The proconsul was astounded. Three times he sent his herald to announce in the midst of the arena, "Polycarp has confessed that he is a Christian!"

No sooner was this announced by the herald than the whole multitude, both pagans and Jews, the entire population of Smyrna, yelled with uncontrolled anger at the top of their voices, "He is the teacher of Asia! The father of the Christians! The destroyer of our gods! He has persuaded many not to sacrifice and not to worship." There arose a unanimous shout that Polycarp should be burned alive.

Now everything happened much faster than it can be told. The mob rushed to collect logs and brushwood from the workshops and the public baths. When the woodpile was ready, Polycarp took off his clothes, removed his belt, and tried to undo his shoes. . . .

The fuel for the pyre was very quickly piled around him. When they wanted to fasten him with nails, he refused. "Let me be. He who gives me the strength to endure the fire will also give me the strength to remain at the stake unflinching, without the security of your nails."

As the fire blazed up around him he prayed one final time: "May I be accepted among their ranks today in thy sight as a rich sacrifice giving thee joy, as a sacrifice which thou hast prepared and revealed beforehand and hast now fulfilled! Thou art the true God in whom there is no falsehood! For everything, therefore, I praise thee. I praise thee; I glorify thee, through the eternal and heavenly high priest, Jesus Christ, thy beloved servant. Through him honor is due to thee and to him and to the Holy Spirit, both now and in all the ages to come. Amen." ⤳

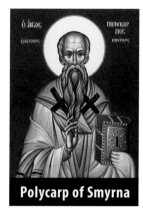

Polycarp of Smyrna

Polycarp's face shone with inward light. He was not in the least disconcerted.

Source: *The Martyrdom of the Holy Polycarp*, ca. AD 156. Translation from Eberhard Arnold, *The Early Christians: In Their Own Words* (Plough, 1997).

Polycarp 2017

JASON LANDSEL

Worldwide, three hundred and twenty-two Christians die for their faith every month, according to the group Open Doors. Their courage mirrors the faith-filled witness of early Christian martyrs such as Polycarp.

Refusing to bow to the gods of Rome, second-century Christians in the Greek city of Smyrna (present-day Izmir, Turkey) were deemed "atheists." In an outbreak of persecution in AD 155, officials dragged Christians into the arena and brutally executed them for public entertainment. Although many were beaten until "the anatomy of the body was visible, even to the veins and arteries," then ripped apart by wild animals or burned alive, they met these trials with such "strength of soul that not one of them uttered a cry or groan."

Disappointed, the mob of spectators called wildly for the blood of a venerable old man named Polycarp, bishop of the church in Asia Minor. Polycarp's exact age at the time is debated, but reports say he had been a Christian for eighty-six years when he heard the news of his impending arrest.

As a young man, Polycarp had been a disciple of the apostle John, and was one of the few remaining who had learned firsthand from those who walked with Jesus. John appointed him to leadership, and in his old age Polycarp was highly esteemed. As Christianity entered its second generation, Polycarp aggressively challenged heresies that threatened to pollute the integrity of its original message. His simple instruction always reflected the clarity of Christ and the apostles.

When the soldiers arrived at his house, Polycarp welcomed them in and prepared them a meal, asking only for an hour to pray. His captors watched as one hour stretched to two, not wishing to interrupt his ardent intercessions for the global church. Then Polycarp was placed on a donkey and led away.

In Smyrna he was hurried to the captain of the local forces, a man named Herod. Inviting Polycarp into his carriage, Herod offered him a chance to survive: "What harm is there in saying, 'Caesar is Lord,' and offering incense?" When Polycarp remained immovable in his faith, Herod angrily threw him from the carriage.

Without looking back, Polycarp got up and marched toward the arena. Over the deafening din inside, he heard a voice speak to him: "Be strong, Polycarp, and play the man." This account, based on the reports of eyewitnesses, gives us the rest:

When he was led forward, the proconsul asked him if he was Polycarp. This he affirmed. The proconsul wanted to persuade him to deny his faith, urging him, "Consider your great age," and all the other things they usually say in such cases. "Swear by the genius of Caesar; change your mind. Say, 'Away with the atheists.'"

Polycarp, however, looked with a serious expression upon the whole mob assembled in the arena. He waved his hand over them, sighed deeply, looked up to heaven, and said, "Away with the atheists."

But the proconsul pressed him further, and

(Continued on preceding page)

Jason Landsel is the artist for Plough's *"Forerunners" series, including the painting opposite.*